Christianity and the Dark Knight, the Unauthorized Guide, is ©2012 by Eric Gaizat

Printed by Lulu.com in the United States of America

Batman and all related characters are property of DC Comics

All rights reserved.

ISBN # 978-1-105-76089-1

Ebook ISBN # 978-1-105-76765-4

"**Who** will rise up for me **against** the wicked? **Who** will take a **stand** for me **against** evildoers?"

- **Psalm 94:16**

Table of Contents:

Foreword by Eric Gaizat: The Hero Inside

For years now, I have wanted to write this book. Several times I talked myself out of it because I was afraid there was not enough interest in the subject. However, after reading a couple of similar books, I came to realize that there is a vast untapped potential to raise up young leaders by reaching them through means that speak directly to them.

I will never forget in the eighth grade, I had a friend who would come to school in a trench coat. Every lunch period he would stop by my table and sit down. Looking around, he would pull out a large red binder and begin flipping through the pages and sell me comic books like it was an illegal substance. He could manage to get his hands on anything I was collecting at the time.

I could not tell you how much lunch money he got from me, but I can tell you that I got some of my most popular and expensive comics that I've purchased to this day. I'd collect all the hottest titles with the first appearances of powerful super villains and heroes that have inspired many of my own characters I would draw in high school. The routine kept going on for over a year until the end of the ninth grade. I kept collecting regularly until I graduated from high school.

My favorite comics of all time have to be the graphic novels of Batman. *The Killing Joke, A Death in the Family, The Dark Knight Returns, The Hush series, Knightfall*, and more, were as inspiring to me as any literature I had ever read in any of my classes. As I got older I began to see the very human side of the characters I was reading about. I actually began to sympathize with heroes and villains alike and began to see reflections in my own life that would inspire me to eventually write this book.

Ultimately it was the release of the 2005 film, *Batman Begins* that ignited the spark inside me to not just evaluate myself, but the entire world around me. I began to see my own faults and strengths from a much clearer perspective. After watching the film, I actually felt a connection to the Bruce Wayne inside myself. His pain, fear, and faith inspired me to "begin," in my own life.

Bruce Wayne's pain and anguish about the death of his parents and the motivation it gave him were all too familiar to me. You see, I lost my grandmother when I was eighteen. My parents had divorced when I was nine, and my grandmother took care of my brother, sister and myself nearly every day until after I graduated high school. Whenever anything bad happened to me, she was there for me and for a while, I thought she was the only one who really cared about me at all. Her name was Irene Eleanor Gaizat. She died of a stroke after being hospitalized for nearly a month. I would stop by and see her sometimes two or three times in a day. As her health deteriorated, so did my faith. On February 26th, she passed away two hours after I had left her. My last words to her were "I'll make you proud of me someday."

And so began my search for God. My mother and grandmother always wanted me to get baptized. I knew that, but what did it mean? What did anything dealing with Christianity mean? I found an old friend of mine and began going to his church nearly 45 minutes away from my house. I went for nearly a year and a half, eventually realizing I was really going to play basketball with my friends afterwards.

No message gave me the inspiration to change my life. I even started shifting my morals toward drugs, alcohol, anger and depression. I would go to my grandmother's grave on the 26th of every month, asking God, why he had to take her from me. I felt very alone and lost, despite my searching for God. It was nearly a year and a half after her death that God answered my longing.

My twin brother found the Indianapolis Church of Christ and was about to be baptized. He invited me out during one of our late night card games with our friends. I told him no and he guilt tripped me into going, because he said that I had agreed to go some time before, but I was too stoned out of my head to realize it.

I got up the next morning with my mom and went to church. I was used to going to an old Baptist church where the average member was about 60 + years old and the sermons were meant for them. When I arrived at my brother's church, I walked in to see so many people all standing and clapping and singing. I was a bit afraid to go in, and someone escorted my family down to the front row, even though I wanted to sit in the back.

Once the sermon got going, the preacher, who was from the affiliated church in Detroit, preached a message entitled, "What are You Waiting For?" It sounded like he was speaking directly to me, calling out my apathy toward seeking God and cutting down my excuses one by one until I had nothing left to stand on. I was impressed. Unfortunately, I was also very lost and confused. I came out to the next midweek and my brother had tricked me into studying the Bible with his mentor (although I would have said yes, had he asked me...) It was at this time I began to learn who God really was and where I was headed unless I got my act together.

I wish I could say I slid smoothly into God's good graces in a matter of days, but that wasn't the case. Even when I did, it would be a long hard road of change and struggle, until I could face my fears and see the hero inside.

Something happened to me that first Sunday morning. I began to take off the blindfold that covered my eyes for the longest time. I was able to look at the world with new eyes and see it for what it really was and still is. I was terrified. I had no hope where I was, and I knew something had to change. My world was about to be turned upside down.

How could one man change the world?

How could I help anyone?

How could I face myself, my fears, and what I had done?

I needed a hero.

It is my hope and intention to draw out the hero inside each one of us. Through examples in the pages of graphic novels, personal stories in the lives of myself and other disciples, and the Bible, I hope to show you that there is a need for those who would go beyond the bounds of mere men, average faith, and conquering both fear and hatred set by those who would hope to see us fall.

We have a hero in this life. He came to us at a time chosen by his father long, long ago. He saved us from our sins and made our lives better. We have to be willing to do whatever it takes to bring others with us as we enter the gates of heaven on the last day.

First we have to awaken the hero within ourselves.

I want to share my life with you. I want to show you what I've seen. I want to show you the world for what it really is. Through the life and actions of one scared little boy who grew to be a warrior for good and guardian of the lives of many, I want you to be inspired. Come with me into the darkness and face your fears. You are ready.

It's time to suit up.

It's time to be who you were meant to be.

And there's no turning back.

Chapter 1: Welcome to Gotham City

Gotham City, before the 1940's, was probably one of the greatest cities known to man. On the outside of the sprawling metropolis, it would have looked like a city of beauty and dignity. People would have marveled at the numerous huge buildings, unbelievable Romanesque statues, and streets paved with a fantastic glow from countless street lamps. Flying overhead, Gotham City must have looked perfect. Rich opportunities for wealth and enrichment of human lives awaited anyone who wished to achieve greatness. To live in this city would have been considered a true blessing.

But somehow... somewhere... something went wrong.

Very wrong.

You see, despite the wondrous glow the city gave, it somehow turned into a great darkness. A depression set in and claimed the jobs, lives, and security of thousands of people. Crime became a way of life. Opportunity gave way to desperation and violence drove many people away. The city no longer had the glow It was meant to have. The city's beauty became a mask, to hide something more hideous. Statues throughout the city stood like guardians of a graveyard and remained a grim reminder of days long passed. Worst of all, the citizens of Gotham lost the three essential qualities needed to make their society work: faith, hope and love. Fear, anger and hate were all that remained. The city seemed bent on self-destruction and intervention itself became the myth.

At some point the city had fallen.

At some point the cries of the helpless and oppressed were thought ignored.

But God heard their cries and sent them a hero.

One late June night, the Wayne family, Thomas, Martha, and their son, Bruce, were coming home after seeing a movie based on Zorro. In the looming shadows, a figure emerged and demanded that they give up their money and valuables. In a struggle, both Thomas and Martha are shot and killed, with their son witnessing the whole thing. The figure escaped into the night and Bruce was left scared, helpless and alone. Fate would have us believe that this child is a victim. Legend would prove Fate wrong because this boy would not become a victim, but would rise to meet his destiny head on and change the fate of his city, becoming a true hero.

Imagine, if you would, that you are working in an office building in Gotham City. Someone runs in and says they've seen Batman outside. What would you do? You'd probably stick your head out the window in hopes to get a glance of the superhero. You might even run outside hoping to meet him.

Now imagine that you lived 2,000 years ago. You are working in your trade shop, probably where your father worked. Someone runs in and tells you Jesus is in town. What would you do? Would you even recognize him? Would he even listen to you? What thoughts would go through your mind?

Do you see the resemblance in these situations? Both require us to look toward true heroes in their trade - the crime fighters looking to Batman and those waiting for the messiah looking to Jesus. Today, some people are still waiting for their hero to enter the scene, to show them the way things should be. They await their hero... their hope.

What are you waiting for?

Many times in the Bible this has happened to God's people. From the beginning, in the Garden of Eden, the world was supposed to be a beautiful, perfect place. Everything had its point and purpose. The world was indeed "good" in God's eyes. But this too was to be short- lived. From the second chapter of Genesis, sin claimed the innocence, splendor, and perfection of God's creation. The world has been in a spiritual battle ever since.

Ravaged lands, slaughtered people, oppressed nations, and selfish causes have claimed much that God has created in this world. Where the innocent still roam, cries have gone to heaven. Many would have us believe that these calls go ignored. But God is sending them a hero.

Can you hear the call?

Do you see the signal?

The time is now.

Gotham City is your city.

Our cities are filled with thousands, maybe even millions of people. We go from day to day without even once asking our neighbors how they are really doing. We fend for ourselves day in and day out. Most people put on a good show. Who thinks to themselves when they see their neighbor, "I wonder if that dad is beating his kids," or, "That lady has been really struggling with her alcoholism." The world tells us we must hide our worst. Those who don't hide it are considered garbage by society. We all have to look good. We are all okay. Don't bring your pain into other people's lives. They don't want to hear about it, so it must not be important. You're not important... and we believe it.

We believe it through apathy, through ignorance, and through the spiritual blindfolds we cling to like a safety blanket. It's easy to believe the lie. It's easy to keep looking the other way. We all feel that we have too much to lose... too much to put on the line. It's easy to think we're too busy. Caring about other people takes effort. We have to be willing to remove of the fear that we will be looked at as strange and different. We have to be more than bystanders, we have to be heroes.

Through the darkness we move to bring forth a beautiful light... a light of hope and a light of truth.

Like Moses, Gideon, and David, who all came to save Israel, so too has a hero come into the city. Faith, hope and love are in short supply and only can someone with those qualities hope to bring it to a befallen people. I am reminded of Jesus when he said in John 10:10,

> "I have come that they may have life, and have it to the full."

Looking around it is not hard to see that the world has fallen. Morals are jeopardized and the pain of those around us is threatening to keep us from becoming who we were meant to be.

Who are you?

What are you searching for inside yourself?

Only you can answer that.

Welcome to the world of Batman.

Are you ready to begin?

Chapter 2: Choices and Consequences

We all make choices every day. This is no mystery. The number of choices we make in a day, for example, are almost uncountable. You made the decision to get up, get dressed, eat something, go to work or school, and those are the big decisions of our day. Turning the pages of this book, reading the next line, finishing the chapter, are examples of small choices. What is the difference in these choices?

Consequences.

When we think of the word consequences, we automatically think of something bad, and rightfully so, most consequences we face are bad. But consequences can be good as well. Choosing to drive slower on the interstate can result in not crashing or getting injured in an accident. That is a good consequence. Reading the Bible and applying it can help us overcome character sins.

On the night of his parent's murder, Bruce Wayne chose to dedicate his life to stopping the evil that made his own life a living nightmare. It would be all too easy to take the road of self-pity, apathy, and anger. Not to say that deep down inside, Bruce wouldn't want to do these things, but he chose to be different than those around him. If he really wanted to make a difference in his life and in the world around him, he must choose what is right, or risk becoming what he hates.

Deep down inside, we must believe in right and wrong, good and evil, light and darkness, God and Satan, and make a choice. Are we the type that tolerates sin in our life, or are we willing to stand up and change the parts of ourselves that keep causing us to fall short? If we can draw the line in our minds, we can clearly see where we are in God's eyes. We can see the line where harmless joking becomes coarse in nature. We can see the point where we stop looking to help and start wanting to hurt. We see love versus lust, anger versus indignation, fear versus caution, and faith versus ignorance. Seeing these things should make it clearer to choose what is right. But does it?

If you said yes, you are a stronger person than I. While it would seem easy to make the right decisions, sin can be tempting. Satan masquerades as an angel of light (2 Corinthians 11:14), and our selfish desires are beacons of want. It's not hard to choose those things. It's not supposed to be. Doing what we're supposed to do... now that's challenging!

As we'll read in the later chapters, in discussing some of Batman's arch-enemies, we will see that there is always the chance to choose what is wrong.

Ultimately, what drives the villains in the comics? Why is there such an unwillingness to repent and choose what is right? We think they're the demons of the comic book pages because they wear strange costumes and have quirky personalities, but I challenge you to see that they are the same people we meet every day. And if they are like us, can't they be saved too?

Why don't they change?

Why don't we?

There are times when sin and circumstances can hit us so hard that we don't think we have choices. Poverty stricken people are more easily drawn to steal to survive or rob to get money. Pregnant girls who feel unready to deal with the consequences of their lust would feel much more likely to have an abortion than to spend the next 20 years of their lives raising a child. You can make a lot more money selling drugs to teenagers than you can working a nine hour day at a restaurant. What makes anyone else so special or different?

The heroes in our lives are the ones who strive to pull themselves out of their situations and change their lives for the better. All they have to do is choose. Choose not to steal; choose to love and raise a child; choose to work and to persevere.

Will it be hard?

Nowhere in the Bible does it say that doing the right thing is easy. But God is standing right next to us. He is rooting for us to choose His way, His fight, His mission, and His path - to be better than those who came before us, and those who choose differently around us.

When Bruce Wayne is sparring against Ducard, his mentor and trainer, in *Batman Begins*, Ducard tells Bruce it is his father who is at fault for his parent's deaths. By failing to act against the evil that threatened them, he sealed both the fate of himself and his wife. Bruce points out that the man had a gun, and Ducard asks if that will stop him in his efforts. Bruce counters with the fact that he has had training. Ducard explains that the training is nothing, without the will to act.

Ducard is right. So many people around us would say that they live as Christians. But what does their life look like? We see pain and suffering around us all the time in people who have been beaten by sin and the challenges in their lives.

Who chooses to fight for them?

Will we be stopped by the pressures of this life to stand and do nothing? We spend so much time learning **how** to conquer the challenges in our lives, but do we act to **defeat** our demons?

Choosing Not to Give Up

In high school, the pressure of fitting in can be so great that those who feel like they have failed are often treated as losers and failures. Often times these are the same individuals who choose to do drugs, to try and make their pains and fears go away.

For many years, I claimed hatred in my heart for the "in crowd" in high school. I had been mistreated, picked on, and pushed around like many people who didn't meet the requirements to be popular. I can remember walking down a hallway in the seventh grade, while an upper classman pushed a pen into my back to make me walk faster.

I can still feel the fear run down my spine as I was picked on in an empty hallway by the schools three biggest bullies with no one to help me. I can still see some of my closest friends being teased for being quiet, having different interests, or was uncompromising in their convictions.

Over the course of early high school, my friends and I began to meet together more often, inside and outside of the classroom. We fashioned ourselves after the knights of the round table, choosing to stand for honor, chivalry, and loyalty. Each one of us was given what was called a ring of honor to wear.

On a necklace of leather string, we each wore a one inch steel ring, with five, smaller, copper rings closed around the bigger ring. Each ring represented an honorable deed we had done, and whenever someone did something honorable, that person would be rewarded with another ring.

I remember when someone would stand up for me, when I was being picked on they almost immediately became a part of our group. Each one was given a ring of honor and our group grew steadily over the next four years. By the end of our senior year, we had well over 20 people in the group, each one loyal to the others no matter what.

You may ask why I am telling you this. I am telling you this because I, too, felt like it would be easy to be a victim of my surroundings. I felt like I was forced to be depressed, angry, and closed in from those around me. I know my friends felt it too. That's why we chose to be different.

We chose to not let the world close in around us, and to stand up for each other. We had our group of knights who would not succumb to drugs, fear, and being pushed around. We chose to be heroes.

We thought our knight status would last forever. Sadly, I can say it did not. After high school, many of us fell into what we tried so hard to steer clear of for so long.

Some cut off our friendships due to petty arguments and some of us fell into drug addiction. Some of us had to deal with messy divorces, depression, loneliness, and loss. Some of our group had even gone to prison for public intoxication, theft, and even murder.

We were no longer heroes.

We became the villains we tried so hard to fight.

Where did we go wrong?

Our choices.

Rather than fight and persevere we, in our own strength, tried to take on our fears and challenges and as we failed, we gave up. It's easier to take the simple way out... to give up on a friendship rather than make it work, forgiving one another.

It's quicker to get drunk and forget your problems than to face them head on. No kingdom can stand against itself... and when we tried, we fell down.

But some of us decided to pick ourselves up.

We chose to fight again.

For some of us who faced addiction, we sought counseling. For those who lost friendships, we made amends. For those who lost parts of our lives we could not get back, we sought to fill those voids with something better.

Are we all where we should be or want to be... no. But that's not the point of the story. We kept fighting. We chose to fight back against the world that told us our lives were over. As for me... I chose God.

It is why I'm here right now telling you this story... to tell you the fight isn't over. Until there is no air to fill my lungs, as long as strength still fills my body, and as long as the cross of Christ stands before me, we will fight on. Not because we want to. Not because we need to... but because we **choose** to.

I choose because I wholeheartedly know I was chosen. (referenced from Matthew 22:14)

No one can take away our freedom to choose.

Paul, the most looked up to Christian in all of history, wrote to the Corinthian church about this very issue of struggling to make the right choices. He says in 2Corinthians 11:22-29:

> *"Are they Hebrews? So am I. Are they Israelites? So am I. Are they Abraham's descendants? So am I. Are they servants of Christ? (I am out of my mind to talk like this.) I am more. I have worked much harder, been in prison more frequently, been flogged more severely, and been exposed to death again and again.*

> *Five times I received from the Jews the forty lashes minus one. Three times I was beaten with rods, once I was stoned, three times I was shipwrecked, I spent a night and a day in the open sea, I have been constantly on the move. I have been in danger from rivers, in danger from bandits, in danger from my own countrymen, in danger from Gentiles; in danger in the city, in danger in the country, in danger at sea; and in danger from false brothers. I have labored and toiled and have often gone without sleep; I have known hunger and thirst and have often gone without food; I have been cold and naked.*

> *Besides everything else, I face daily the pressure of my concern for all the churches. Who is weak, and I do not feel weak? Who is led into sin, and I do not inwardly burn?"*

We all choose the paths we walk down every day and we must face the consequences, good or bad, to whatever end. Paul didn't stop choosing the path of Jesus because he fell down or faced hardships even to the point of death. In fact, it was because of Jesus and his love for others he kept going. We have to do the same.

Just because we make the right choices does not mean that our lives will be easier. Paul's life sure wasn't. But we know our lives will be better. When we fall, we can choose to stop and stay down or we can choose to get back up and hang on until we stand firm against the world once more.

Just like Paul.

Just like Batman.

The Bible says many things about the choices we make. In James 4:17, the Bible says:

> *"Anyone, then, who knows the good he ought to do and doesn't do it, sins."*

God tells us there is good to do in this world. We see it every day, whether it be helping someone in need, encouraging each other daily, or challenging a dominant sin in our own life.

Some of us are still struggling to make the choice to become Disciples of Christ in our lives. What are we waiting for, I wonder? Is it the tempting nature of the world? Is it the guilt of past sins? Is it the fear that we're giving up on a fun and eventful life, and becoming more like our parents? Do we want to be accepted so much by those around us that the fear of losing that is all we've dedicated ourselves to living for? What are you allowing to stand in your way?

You cannot overcome it unless you are willing to act. You must be ready to fight, just like Bruce was going to have to step outside his door every night, for the city he loved in his heart, we have to be willing to step outside of ourselves to become more than just mere men in the eyes of our opponent, the world.

We will never fit in and we should never **want** to. To choose the path of the world is to choose defeat after defeat and to expect the consequences that follow. Only when we choose God's path will we find victory.

Batman is different because he **chooses** to act. He **chooses** to fight evil. He **chooses** to put on the costume every night, knowing it may be his last, because he believes in his fight so much that he is willing to lay down his life to make his city a better place. He has hope that when people see his example, they may choose to stand by his side and go down the narrow path.

The path of the hero.

The path of God.

Do you see your world as a place worth fighting for? Are you willing to lay down your own ambitions in this life to make it a better one for everyone to live in? We can all be heroes, dedicated to the task of fighting the evil in our lives. All we have to do is make the choice.

I leave you this scripture in Joshua 24:15:

*"...then **choose** for yourselves this day whom you will serve, whether the gods your forefathers served beyond the River, or the gods of the Amorites, in whose land you are living. But as for me and my household, we will serve the LORD."*

You cannot move forward unless you choose to do so. Like Batman chose to pick himself up and train for the war ahead of him, you too must choose the path you will face for the rest of your life.

God chooses us.

What do we choose?

Chapter 3: Suiting Up – Assessing Your Spiritual Gifts

"He knew that criminals, by nature, were a cowardly and superstitious lot. In turn, he donned a cape and cowl and became a creature of the night, preying on those who broke the law. They now call him the Batman."

Alfred Pennyworth- *"Batman: Hush"* [a]

Our Utility Belt

Compared to the other members of the Justice League, Batman should feel out of his league. He doesn't have any super powers. No flight, no super speed, no super strength, no invulnerability, no magic rings, or even the desire to have such gifts. What makes Batman so unique and special is that without the flashy powers, he still manages to be one of the greatest heroes of all time, because he is a normal person, just like you and me.

Bruce Wayne traveled the world in search of the perfect training that he would need to combat crime. He learned foreign languages to be able to translate and go undercover when he needed to catch foreign criminals.

He honed his strength to be at its peak, and pushed his body to the limits. He trained under the greatest of masters to learn fighting, escaping, and the art of invisibility. He learned to master his fear and become a terrifying stalker of the night.

Training his mind to understand logic, chemistry, physics, math, forensics, and investigation, he would not stop until he became the world's greatest detective. Ultimately, he refuses to let any part of him go to waste, utilizing every aspect of his being, pushing himself to every conceivable limit, so that he cannot say that he had not done everything in his power to make a difference.

Using his family's company, he would create and use the latest technologies to help wage his war on crime, so that he could be ready for anything. In the end, no one else on Earth could be Batman. No living person has the same will, desire, perseverance, knowledge, and drive to use all these things to fight the evil that has enveloped his city.

Why did he do all this? What did he hope to accomplish by sacrificing his own personal interests for several years to learn all these things? What was his ultimate goal, and does he ever achieve it? Wouldn't it be easier to just move out of Gotham and leave it to its fate?

In a town that seems bent on destroying itself, fighting to maintain order in a world of chaos would seem at the very least impossible. What does Batman have that trumps all his other gifts and utilities that help him wage war?

Faith.

Batman has faith that his deeds, his actions, his fight, will not fall on deaf ears or on unmovable hearts. In *Batman Begins*, the whole movie is set around Bruce being told that he cannot accomplish change in Gotham, and that his parents were an obvious example of this fact.

Carmine Falcone tells him he will always be afraid, Ra's al Ghul tells him no one can save Gotham. Jim Gordon feels like they are alone in the fight. Everyone else is without faith, but Bruce does not give in. He knows that for every instance he falls, it provides him with the opportunity to learn from his mistakes, pick himself up and keep fighting. As long as he fights, the city will have hope.

For years, Thomas Wayne tried to fight poverty and injustice in Gotham, but only in his death would he motivate the rich and powerful into action to save their city. Bruce is ultimately the one who is motivated the most to do so. Why would I say that?

Let's look at a similar example in the Bible. In Luke 21, the old woman gives two little pieces of copper to the temple treasury. Other people gave substantial amounts into the offering box, but she gave from faith that what she gave would be returned to her by God. The rich in Gotham gave money to get the city by, but

Bruce is willing to die and fight to inspire the people to take their city back. The poorest person to the richest, not just one class. If Gotham is going to save itself from its own destruction, everyone must join in the fight.

It is no different in this world. How can society save itself? Most "Christians" can't even agree on what it takes to be saved, and spend so much time arguing about it, that the graves keep getting filled every day with those who are truly lost.

Lost because the war hasn't stopped. We have. It won't stop until God decides mankind gets no more days to figure it out. There are still so many people, just walking around the battlefield, oblivious that they're walking into a mine field, spiritually.

That's where the real heroes come in.

We must be willing to swoop in and save the day. We have to be willing to extend our arms to those people who have stepped off the cliff and right into the arms of the enemy... and make no mistake, there is an enemy. But are we willing, like Batman, to give our very lives if necessary, to inspire the people to retake their lives before it is too late?

How do we fight back? What tools do we have at our disposal? How can we be like Batman in these areas? First we have to see what it is we have to work with. Let's open our utility belt and see the tools we've been given. After all, our Father's "company" has spared no expense in giving us these gifts.

I am talking about our spiritual gifts. The first question we have to ask ourselves is what are our gifts? If you don't know, don't panic. Just ask those in your ministry, your parents or friends what they think your strengths are.

Is it something artistic? Can you play an instrument, draw and paint, sculpt, or interpret what others create? Do you have the ability to make friends easily? Are you personable or a natural leader? Do people seem to be drawn to you charismatically? Do you empathize with others and give good advice? What about skills?

Can you understand computers, programming, gaming or business? Do you learn languages easily? Are you a sports all-star? Do you excel in one particular sport or are you getting picked first for every event you play? Maybe you just don't hit the panic button when things go haywire around you.

There are, of course, an unlimited number of possibilities. God has so many gifts he gives to us; we barely know where to begin sometimes in deciphering where we excel the most. In asking other people, we can gain a better understanding of our strengths, by removing our personal feelings from the situation.

Paul, when writing to the Corinthian church, described these gifts, or tools to help others:

> *"There are different kinds of gifts, but the same Spirit. There are different kinds of service, but the same Lord. There are different kinds of working, but the same God works all of them in all men.*
>
> *Now to each one the manifestation of the Spirit is given for the common good. To one there is given through the Spirit the message of*

wisdom, to another the message of knowledge by means of the same Spirit, to another faith by the same Spirit, to another gifts of healing by that one Spirit, to another miraculous powers, to another prophecy, to another distinguishing between spirits, to another speaking in different kinds of tongues, and to still another the interpretation of tongues. All these are the work of one and the same Spirit, and he gives them to each one, just as he determines.

Now you are the body of Christ, and each one of you is a part of it. And in the church God has appointed first of all apostles, second prophets, third teachers, then workers of miracles, also those having gifts of healing, those able to help others, those with gifts of administration, and those speaking in different kinds of tongues. Are all apostles? Are all prophets? Are all teachers? Do all work miracles? Do all have gifts of healing? Do all speak in tongues? Do all interpret? But eagerly desire[e] the greater gifts." (1 Corinthians 12:4-11,27-31)

What good would it do Batman if he only used his batarangs or only his grappling hook? He wouldn't be quite as effective as he would really want to be. He needs to be able to speak in several languages, use a variety of tools, and fight in martial arts style to achieve his goals. As a ministry, our gifts are just as important.

Some people are leaders, some teachers, and some have unusual abilities that can help people come closer to God. We are each important in the fight, and we have to use the gifts we're given wisely to help as many as possible. Sometimes we find that we have gifts in areas we had no idea about, simply because we try to be like others to win them to Christ. Maybe you're an excellent basketball player but didn't know it until you played with a guy you were reaching out to, all because you wanted to relate better to him. It can work in several other areas of our lives, but we just have to be willing to be used, without limitation to help others.

If you aren't sure how to use your gifts to win others, talk to your ministry leader. They may have suggestions you never thought of, that can greatly increase the impact you are trying to have on your school, job or wherever your battlefield lies. After all, if Batman hadn't sought out the world's greatest minds to teach him, then how effective would his skills be?

Let me give you an example. If you are good at writing poetry, then have a poetry night inviting both disciples and non-disciples so that you can reach out to people with similar interests. After all, if they can see someone like them as a true Christian, why can't they become a Christian like you? Get creative and God can help you bring more people to the faith than you realized possible.

Donning Our Costume

Batman's costume gives him much protection as he ventures out into the night. His body armor protects him against many types of bullets and knives. His mask shields his face, protecting not only his skull but his identity from being discovered by his foes. It also gives him the ability to see infrared, so that he can detect his prey in low visibility situations. His "bat ears" are radio receivers and he can hear what the police hear throughout Gotham so that he can be there in a moment's notice. His cape helps him glide across the night sky. His utility belt holds all of his expensive gadgets and makes them all accessible in an instant. His gloves and boots are armor plated to give him resistance to cheap attacks and suffering easily avoidable injuries.

Let's not be naïve. We are using our gifts as tools. We use the Bible as a sword. (Hebrews 4:12-13) But did you know that we also have spiritual armor? It's true.

And it's not that different than donning a superhero's costume. In Ephesians 6:10-18, the Bible says:

"Finally, be strong in the Lord and in his mighty power. Put on the full armor of God so that you can take your stand against the devil's schemes. For our struggle is not against flesh and blood, but against the rulers, against the authorities, against the powers of this dark world and against the spiritual forces of evil in the heavenly realms. Therefore put on the full armor of God, so that when the day of evil comes, you may be able to stand your ground, and after you have done everything, to stand.

Stand firm then, with the belt of truth buckled around your waist, with the breastplate of righteousness in place, and with your feet fitted with the readiness that comes from the gospel of peace. In addition to all this, take up the shield of faith, with which you can extinguish all the flaming arrows of the evil one. Take the helmet of salvation and the sword of the Spirit, which is the word of God. And pray in the Spirit on all occasions with all kinds of prayers and requests. With this in mind, be alert and always keep on praying for all the saints."

Our armor protects us from the devil's schemes. Our costume protects us from the invisible forces of darkness that we can't even see that try to manipulate our actions and direct us into the path of sin and despair. But just like Batman, we must actively put on our armor.

How well would Batman fare if he left the cave without his chest piece? Or without his mask? He would leave himself wide open to attacks. In the same way, we have to be ready to suit up against the war we face here on our turf.

It's not enough to put on your helmet of salvation, but forget your shield. By doing so, we openly invite Satan to take his best shot with his flaming arrows of sin and conquer our faith. If we forget our belt of truth, we can unfortunately get caught with our pants down in lies and betrayal. In the same way, if we leave our sword at home we can defend all we like but we will never be able to win against our foes.

To illustrate this point further, how often do we leave our Bibles at home or not carry them with us? Do we leave it at home when we go to work? What about at school? What about to church or devotionals? If we don't take our Bibles with us wherever we go, how can we fight against the lies of those who would undermine our faith or challenge those who we are reaching out to?

By not having our "sword" handy whenever we need it, we are simply standing on the battlefield with no defense. We will not conquer evil.

Having our Bible is not the same as wielding it properly either.

I encourage you to read the Bible through all the way. At times it is difficult. Some passages mean more to us than others, but that does not make them any less important. Some things we have to discover for ourselves. You can read three chapters a day and get through the whole Bible in less than a year.

Coming out of the waters of baptism, I can remember telling my brother that our circle of friends from high school, those we were the closest to, would follow our path quickly because they would trust us and see the difference in our lives. This sadly was not the case.

Openly sharing my faith with my best friends was a complete disaster. I was shut down, ignored, told off, and rejected by every single one of them. I was shocked at their total denial of what I had experienced. Not one of them was willing to give what I had learned a shot. Even worse, they challenged my faith with so many questions it left my head spinning. It was then that I not only felt very alone but clueless as to why I believed what I believed.

Like Bruce Wayne in *Batman Begins*, I had to leave my old life to learn the ways of understanding. Bruce left Gotham because it was the only way for him to see what it was like to be a criminal to understand their thinking. I had to leave my friends and their influences to study my faith completely so no one could tell me I was brainwashed or ignorant of my beliefs.

For two years I studied the scriptures from front to back. I took classes on the Bible and learned the context you would need to tear down many spiritual arguments. My favorite one is that the Bible is full of contradictions, which I strongly disagree with. (Anyone who wants to prove me wrong had better be able to have scriptures and context to back it up with!)

I loved the fact that every day I went into my Bible class my core beliefs were challenged and that I walked away stronger than ever. It wasn't easy though. I remember one girl getting up from her seat crying. She left the class forever, because she was challenged deeply about her faith. I even had to refocus on my other classes because my grades were slipping due to my zeal for the scriptures.

After my two year hiatus from my friends, I returned ready to face their questions and accusations. While I love them dearly, they didn't deserve the absence of my friendship while I took my leave. I simply needed to remove myself from their influence so that they could not sway my convictions because of my sympathy to their situations.

I had to don my costume and know its purposes to be able to stand my ground. Many times on campus I needed my armor and many times I prevailed because I was ready for the fight. I was kicked out of campus Christian groups because of my unwavering belief in baptism.

I had people tell the visitors of my Bible-talk that my church was a cult and to stop coming to our events. I was once in a large room that erupted in a heated debate on speaking in tongues. Without my armor, sword, and gifts, there is no way I would have made it through many of these events.

We have to be ready for the war that is raging around us.

The only way to do that is to get suited up.

What do you believe? Why? Is it because your parents told you to believe it? Or is there more to your faith than that? Could an atheist tear down your faith? Why or why not? Can you honestly say that your faith is backed up by specific scriptures?

You will face these challenges from the opposition.

It's not a matter of why, but when.

If you don't own a notebook, get one. Put in it the things you learn. Write down topical studies or the context of what you are reading and how it can apply to others so that when you are challenged by non-believers you can stand your ground. We don't get a day off to be ignorant. We have to put on our full armor or else we're sitting ducks.

Remember, a soldier doesn't just defend but fights to gain ground.

With our sword and armor God gives us we can be like Batman and press on defeating foe after foe no matter how gritty the battles get because we have faith that this world can be different. Our school, our jobs, our classrooms, and our families can be won. We just have to be willing to act, use our powers, don our costume, and then become the heroes we so often read about.

Now that we're suited up, get ready to head into the battlefield.

The night awaits.

Chapter 4: The Mission – Journey into the Night

<u>Confronting the Darkness Within</u>

Ever since the night Thomas and Martha Wayne were murdered, Bruce knew his childhood was over. Every family he saw having fun and being together tore at his soul and served as a reminder of everything he had lost. What child would understand the pain and torment he felt?

Which child could relate with the desire for revenge and anger that he had to deal with as they played on the playground? How many times did he picture the showdown between himself and his parents' killer? When that day came, what would he do?

In *Batman Begins* we can learn a lot about the things that Bruce Wayne felt and experienced that started his journey into becoming a hero of legend. He harbored feelings of guilt, anger and vengeance well into his college years. When he found out his parents' killer was going free, he decided to make his move.

Armed with a pistol outside the courtroom, he waited for his killer to emerge so that he could finally bring his suffering to an end. Would Joe Chill say anything? Would he die as fast as his parents had? What kind of pressure would he finally feel lifted from his shoulders?

Bruce was trembling and angry as his parents' murderer was exiting the building in his direction. Just as Bruce went to make his move, a woman working for Falcone, the head mob boss of the city, shot Chill in the chest, killing him in front of Bruce.

As his friend Rachel urged Bruce to leave, he refused, wanting to watch vengeance play itself out. He should have been happy to see Chill die... something was wrong. Bruce was still empty inside.

All those years of planning his revenge spilled away with every drop of blood that came from Joe Chill's wounds. He would never have his revenge. It was taken from him. When Rachel found out what he was planning to do, she told him his father would be ashamed of his actions, and rightfully so.

Thomas Wayne was always remembered for saving lives not taking them away. Confused and alone, Bruce ran into the night tormented by the demons that surrounded him.

How could he find peace?

When would the hurting stop?

Looking at the gun he was going to use to kill Chill, he remembered the fear he had staring down the barrel of the gun that killed his parents and he realized he was just another coward with a gun. Throwing it into the harbor, he went to confront Falcone in the bar he always hung out in. He would show Falcone that he wasn't afraid of him... but he was wrong.

Falcone literally had the city bought and paid for. He was a god among men and he could take or destroy anything he wanted and there was nothing Bruce could do about it. Next, Falcone tells Bruce that just because he had lost his parents it didn't mean that he understood the evil the world could hold.

Falcone's words ring true to most "Christians" in this world. I use the term loosely because so many people are either ignorant or so hypocritical about God and his ways, that I can't take them seriously and neither would Satan. I can say that because I used to be one of them.

So many people in the world try to dismiss the devil completely or to pretend he is a weak evil spirit. By doing so only plays into his hands. We shouldn't be afraid of him, but we shouldn't underestimate him either. Bruce didn't think he was afraid of Falcone until he gave him something to be afraid of... losing those he was close to.

Bruce underestimated him.

Confronting Falcone was a disaster. Not only did he not flinch at Bruce's stand, but he showed him that his misunderstanding of the downtrodden and criminals of Gotham would make him a slave forever to fear.

Bruce left Gotham to understand.

Running with criminals, he began to realize the harsh world they lived in but he never let himself become one of them. He didn't lose his goal but when he finally got thrown into a prison he didn't know where else to go. That's when someone looked down on him and decided it was time to move in the right direction.

And I don't mean Ra's al Ghul.

When I first started searching for God it was because I had lost my grandmother. I was depressed and mourned the fact that no one in my life seemed to understand my pain and help me overcome it.

I thought by going to church with an old friend it would make things magically better. It didn't. I had no idea what I was getting myself into. How could I fight an enemy if I didn't even know who it was or what I was doing?

You see, like Bruce I was entering a world I didn't understand. No one tried to sit down with me and study the Bible. I was a naive 19 year old wearing a black trench coat hanging out with a bunch of teenagers who, as far as I could see, were just like every teenager I had ever met.

Like Bruce, my inner desire to understand God kept me from going down the same path as many of the teenagers I was hanging around. But I still wasn't conquering sin in my life. I was fighting Satan like Bruce was fighting crime.

Poorly.

Only when I was truly broken would I begin to look for the path that God had for me. I would be able to face my opponent and not back down and after having done everything... to stand. (Ephesians 6:13)

The Training Begins

Bruce ends up meeting his trainer, a man named Ducard, later to be known as Ra's al Ghul. Ra's has a path for Bruce. One that would help him shape his destiny forever to become the man he always knew he needed to be.

In Bruce's cell, Ducard tells him that he's discovered his identity despite Bruce's attempts to keep that information secret. Ducard tells him that he's got a vision for his life, a path that can lead him to what he has been searching for.

Ducard shares a great secret with Bruce that no matter how much he has dedicated himself to understanding criminals, Bruce has become truly lost in his scramble to find justice. Ducard sees the potential in Bruce, even if he can't see it in himself.

Ducard tells Bruce three steps to realizing the full potential locked within. Something that Christians wanting to change the world could learn. First, you have to make yourself more than just a man. Second, devote yourself to an ideal. Thirdly, if they (your enemies) can't stop you, **then** you become the legend you seek to be.

To a spiritual superhero, these steps are very true. Paul once told the Corinthian church that when they argued, they made themselves out to be 'mere men'. To Satan, our persecutors, and the powers of darkness, we have to become more than just men in the minds of our opponents. This means we have to believe we can be darkness's worst nightmare. (Even demons, in Acts 19:15, knew about Paul and what he was capable of.)

Second, you have to devote yourself to the ideal. That ideal is Christianity and Christ's teachings. If you haven't read the whole Bible all the way through, then how can you stand your ground against your enemies, who will not take you seriously if you aren't even aware of your own scriptures. Read the Bible. Apply it, and watch your life and actions begin to count for something and reshape the world you see around you.

Lastly, and this is on the part of God more than you: If the powers of darkness can't stop you, and your faith pushes you beyond the realm of your influence, then you can impact not just your world, but **the** world.

You just have to believe you can, have the courage to try, and develop your specific strategy to overcoming the darkness and shape your goals. If it is God's will for you to impact the hearts and minds of your people, then it will be done regardless of your own actions because God will see it through.

Back to my story, after my grandmother died, I was a man looking for a path. Where I ended up though, was lost in the middle of nowhere. Satan was right. I didn't understand what I was trying to do. Was I out to just play basketball with my friends or did I really care about saving my soul... and the souls of those I cared about? Whatever my original intentions... I was truly lost.

Like Ducard, coming to teach Bruce the path of purpose, it wasn't until my mentor and friend Tim Kirk actually opened the Bible, challenged me, and helped me to change, did I find the courage and excitement that my life could be different. Tim knew I was searching for God but he couldn't make me walk the path.

Only I could know what it was I was looking for. No one could tell me. What about you? Do you feel like you've been spoon-fed the Christian life by your parents since before you can remember? Do you feel like it's just not for you or that it doesn't appeal to you on your level? No one can tell you what you refuse to listen to. Only you can know why you're here.

If you died today, could you honestly say you would go to heaven? Why? Because that is what your minister told you? Or can you back it up with scripture? Can you do it off the top of your head or do you fumble through the pages in a scramble just to prove me wrong?

The path of the disciple is a narrow one. Only a few find it. Stray even just a little and you end up on a path of destruction like so many who have come before you. (Matthew 7:13-14)

Are you ready to begin taking this world back from him who would see us all fail? You have to understand sin to conquer it. You must be willing to face the darkest part of yourself before you can face the darkness of the world.

You can't be afraid of falling. It's what the journey is all about. Every time we fall we have a savior who is there to pick us up again, dust us off and ask us: "What is it you were looking for?"

Only we can answer that.

Who are you?

If you want to face the world you must first journey inward. Face your fears and challenge what's inside you. You can do it. Who do we want to be inside? What keeps us from becoming the hero we bury deep within ourselves to conform to the world's standards? Bruce Wayne knew he could not fight crime as himself because he knew criminals would not fear him. We cannot face sin without the faith it takes to be more than mere men.

Imagine if you will, Bruce Wayne's first night as Batman. This is where the rubber meets the road. In the cold rain of the night, where does he go? In which direction does he turn? How does he know he'll even come upon a crime? If he takes a bullet his first night out, does he cease to be heroic? If he dies on the wet streets, fighting his first criminal, has he failed?

In the story "*Batman: Year One*," Batman is hiding from Commissioner Gordon who is trying to catch him. He sees a woman about to get hit by a car. Batman has a choice: Save the woman and be discovered or hide and let the woman die. He decides his safety comes second to helping someone in need. Even if it means giving himself up. Dying does not mean failure. Doing nothing does.

Batman knows his enemies will fear him. He has chosen his costume well. He blends in with shadow and makes himself more in the mind of his opponent than he really is. He is Batman. He will fight crime, make a difference, and take the city back. There can be no other outcome.

In the scene of *Batman Begins* where he is flying back to Gotham, he and Alfred begin discussing what Bruce's plans are for returning to Gotham. Alfred recalls that Bruce's parents nearly bankrupted Wayne Enterprises trying to help people. It was their death though that ultimately shocked the wealthy and powerful into action.

Bruce brings a deep truth into the light when he says that people need dramatic examples to shake them out of their apathy. As a man, Bruce was flesh and blood, he could be ignored or destroyed. But as a symbol he could be incorruptible, and everlasting.

Bruce invents his new persona. It will be the face Gotham will look to when it needs help. He will be incorruptible. Crime has a new enemy.

What about you? Who are you? Do you hate sin in your life so much that you are willing to do anything to get rid of it? To get rid of sin, Jesus even tells us in Matthew 5:29-30:

"If your right eye causes you to sin, gouge it out and throw it away. It is better for you to lose one part of your body than for your whole body to be thrown into hell. And if your right hand causes you to sin, cut it off and throw it away. It is better for you to lose one part of your body than for your whole body to go into hell."

Can we get dramatic with the sin in our lives? It may be the only way we make it to heaven.

Sometimes people need dramatic examples to make them look for God. I did. The loss of my grandmother felt like it was too much to bear, but God knew that it is what it would take to make me seek him. Would I struggle with that decision?

Absolutely, but we'll discuss that later in this book. The point for now is that I didn't give up searching for the answers that made me who I am today.

What dramatic example does God have to show you to make you seek him and take him seriously? We can choose to know God before disaster strikes, but will we?

What about the people you know in your life? When tragedy strikes their lives, do they turn to you for comfort? Can you use your knowledge of God to help them and show them the true path of a God who hates injustice and sin and is willing to heal them? All we have to do is open our mouths and show those in our lives that we are the heroes of this generation.

God believes in us.

Do we?

How can we help others find the path if we ourselves are not on it?

I encourage you to sit down and examine yourself to see where you are spiritually. Don't lie to yourself. God knows the truth and so do you. Then look at the scriptures and see what awaits you there.

There are scriptures to teach, to correct, to train, to rebuke, give us guidance to make us stronger, and make us into the heroes God wants us to be. (2Timothy 3:16-17)

This world is a dark place. Satan is its Lord. People are stumbling and falling down with no one to help them up. So many are filled with the indescribable feeling that no one cares and that there is no God listening to their pleas... They are wrong.

God has sent a hero.

A hero inside you.

Be that dramatic example to shake them out of apathy.

People want to be saved, and they want to be loved. Don't give up on them. It would be all too easy for Bruce Wayne to move to another city and let Gotham destroy itself. Only faith can keep him from falling victim to the apathy that comes with those who have no hope. Bruce Wayne is not a villain. Bruce Wayne is not a bystander. He is a hero. He will fight to save those he loves from the darkness that threatens to overcome the world he knows can exist.

Will there be opposition? Yes. On a daily basis it seems Batman takes on one of his hundreds of opponents, each with the same hope that if he reaches but one of his villains and helps them change their life, his struggle was worth it. Your struggle is no different.

It's okay to feel overwhelmed sometimes. It's during these times Satan is trying to convince us we've failed. God tells us he will not give us more than we can bear but we have to see the way through and hang on to our faith until we are victorious. (1Corinthinas 10:13)

Dick Grayson, during Grant Morrison's run on the death and return of Bruce Wayne, took up the mantle of the

Batman. While doing so, he had these incredible words to reflect on:

> "You know what? Some people don't want to be saved because saving means changing. And changing is always harder than staying the same.
>
> It takes courage to face yourself in the mirror and look beyond the reflection. To find the you that you should have been. The you who got derailed by cruel childhood events. Events that took your life's natural trajectory and twisted it.
>
> Changing it into something unimaginable... or even incredible... giving you the courage to embrace your birthright, your destiny, and finally realize...
>
> that you are Batman." [b]

You're worth it. Don't give in to the darkness and give up on your hopes as a true Christian. You're not alone. Even when you can't see anyone else around to help you, God is cheering you on, telling you that he loves you and that he is right there. We just have to choose not to give up and bring the light back into the darkness.

Chapter 5: Dynamic Duo – Now we're two...

"The Batman needed a Robin...I guess the truth is that I was lonely... didn't want to go it alone."

-Batman – "A Death in the Family" [c]

More than a Duo

For many years, Batman has been portrayed as a loner. The dark dreary cape and cowl, fighting crime, putting fear in criminals - everything was going according to Bruce Wayne's plan. To capture this element, the films *Batman*, *Batman Returns*, and *Batman Begins* were all based on the caped crusader fighting crime on his own. In the comics it was the same for many years since his creation in the 1930's.

Everyone is familiar with the boy wonder, Robin and the example that the dubbed "Dynamic Duo" set for years to come. Robin though, is not the only crime fighting partner Batman has had throughout the years. In fact, he has gained a strong following in Gotham, by those who have taken the same vow to rid the city of evil.

Some of Batman's allies include Commissioner Jim Gordon and his daughter Barbara Gordon also known as Batgirl, who took on the role of partner for Batman for some time. Alfred, Bruce's butler is his longest confidant, helping to encourage Bruce whenever situations become burdensome for the super-hero.

Tim Drake, the third Robin, became Bruce's apprentice to learn how to fight crime and become the world's greatest detective. Leslie Thompkins, the woman who reached out to Bruce the night his parents were killed, has been there to comfort Bruce in many times of despair. Even Catwoman, also known as Selina Kyle, has been part of Bruce's life and shown him how to let down his guard and to love.

For a loner, Bruce has quite a long list of partners. These are only a few of his closer friends, not to mention Superman, the new Batgirl, the Huntress, Azrael and everyone in the Justice League. Although most people would define Batman as being a loner, they would be wrong.

Bruce's sense of loyalty to his friends has brought him more allies than he would have dreamed possible. For the purposes of this chapter though, we'll look at those closest to him.

Since the beginning of Batman's career he has sought friendship and partnership with the Commissioner of the City, Jim Gordon. In *Batman Begins*, even before Bruce has finished his costume, he seeks out the help of one of Gotham's last good cops.

Sneaking into his office and holding him seemingly at gunpoint (although he is only using a stapler), he reveals his plans and recruits Gordon into his plan to bring peace to Gotham. At the end of their conversation Jim realizes that Bruce is alone and asks, "You're just one man?" Bruce boldly replies, "Now we're two."

There is a certain truth in what Bruce is trying to convey to Jim. It is going to be a long hard road to lead Gotham out of its troubles. But if one man with a vision and the courage to stand for what is right can spread that message to just one person, they can change the destiny of an entire city.

No one man can do it alone. If Bruce wants to motivate the citizens of Gotham to save their city, he has to spread his message.

The Bible says quite a bit about companions and doing what's right. Several times Jesus tells his disciples to go out in pairs through the various towns to spread the gospel. (Mark 6:7) Jesus even tells them that wherever two or more are gathered in his name, he is there. (Matthew 18:20) God tells Adam and Eve that it is not good for a man to be alone but through marriage, they can depend on each other and give each other strength. (Genesis 2:18) In Ecclesiastes 4:12, it is written:

> *"Though one may be overpowered, two can defend themselves. A cord of **three strands** is not quickly broken."*

We are meant to look to each other for comfort and support. That is why there are so many "one another" scriptures in the Bible. This is ultimately, I think, why Bruce Wayne trained Dick Grayson to be his partner, the infamous Robin.

When Bruce saw Dick and his pain he saw the chance for someone to finally understand what he went through in his own life and share his way of coping with the pain. Robin's brighter colors truly marked the lighter side of Bruce's life and a chance for him to let innocence back into his life.

Who is your sidekick? Who do you want to pass your torch to and share in the struggles with more than anyone else? We're supposed to be united in heart and purpose, spreading the gospel like Batman is trying to spread hope through Gotham.

The difference is that our hope is not in a hero that can be killed or ignored but in a savior who has surpassed centuries of dispute and persecution. With a savior like that it's not hard to spread the word. All we have to do is believe in what we're doing and open our homes, our mouths, and our lives.

Our Partners in the Fight

My partner in the gospel has to be my twin brother, Chris. He is the one who first challenged me to come to church and open the Bible. He is the one who shares with me the same sense of loyalty and commitment to God that I've not experienced with anyone else I've ever met.

We have this connection that surpasses words with an almost unspoken knowledge of how to work together. To say that he was my only ally, though, would be ridiculous.

There are several people in my life who I hold in a kind of "team" status. At different levels I have teachers, like the pastor who helped me learn how to speak publicly and help with some of my hardest times of sin, or the men who studied the scriptures with me and helped me become a Christian.

They challenged me to my core when I was at my lowest and I'm grateful for their teaching and guidance. It is their continuing faith in me that inspires my own.

Then there are those who are more involved with me on a daily basis and help me through my every day battles. These are my closest companions and without them and their challenges to keep me open and humble,

I would no doubt fall back into the sin that overwhelmed me before I was a Christian. The loyalty that we have for each other gives me the confidence to be open and honest with how I'm really doing.

Next there are those who I am helping to become Christians, mostly in my teen ministry at the moment. I enjoy the teacher/student relationships and am honored at the chance to help them make better decisions than those who came before them.

I respect them for their decisions to become Christians at a much harder time in their lives than when I came around. Watching the teens in my ministry change their lives for the better make me feel like I've gained new allies and sidekicks.

Lastly, there are the people in the world that I am reaching out to. I see the heroes in them and try to give them the vision both God and I have for their lives. Reaching out to my friends outside of church helps me to remember where I have come from and sometimes serve as examples of the consequences of the choices we make in our lives if we choose to make them without God. I know the joy of overcoming sin and Satan's plan for my life and I am ready to share that with anyone who is willing to listen.

In Batman's life he also has the same level of friends and companions. Without them he cannot hope to save the city, and worse yet, he would probably lose himself in his own darkness and sorrow. He has a vision for each of his teammates that surpasses where they are now. He sees them maturing into what they were meant to be.

For example, in the graphic novel *Hush*, Batman had this to say about Dick Grayson, also known as Nightwing:

> *"Through the years, I've debated whether or not it was fair of me to take him in. Train him. But I've learned that Dick wasn't like me. He didn't come from a world of privilege. He was a performer. Gifted in that way. And while, at the time, the transition from Robin to Nightwing was... difficult for us both... it was a day I had long prepared myself for because...*
>
> *Dick was born to be in the center ring."* [d]

Later, in that same story, Batman had this to say about Tim Drake, the current Robin:

> *"Tim clung to a theory that Batman needs a Robin. More than just for a legacy, but as a balance. I had taken both Dick and Jason in when they had no place else to go. But Tim sought out the role. He wanted to be Robin. And as hard as I tried to convince him otherwise, Tim worked for it.*
>
> *Dick saw being Robin as a thrill. It's probably why he outgrew it. Jason saw being Robin as a game. It's probably what got him killed. But Tim, I have to hand it to the boy, he wants to be the world's*

greatest detective. And from what I've seen so far... he will be someday." [e]

Batman's vision for his partners helps his drive not just as a leader but as a friend who wants to see them succeed in life. If Batman can encourage ten people to fight evil then those ten encourage ten and so on, how long will it take to retake Gotham from the corrupt. It will take time, maybe more than Bruce has left to live, but he can ignite the flame inside each person he lets into the "cave" he calls his life and spark a revolution against evil.

Sound familiar?

Jesus was trying to do the exact same thing. By choosing his apostles and letting them into his life and helping them, training them, fighting with them and dying in front of them, he sparked a revolution that would change the face of the world forever. He showed his disciples the way to get to heaven. His words have traveled this far and this long to you.

What will you do with them?

Jesus' great commission in Matthew 28:18-20 shows us that even at the time when Jesus was about to send his disciples out, that some of them doubted. It's okay to struggle with the truth from time to time but we have to keep pushing what we know is right and through those hard times we will know that Jesus is with us every step of the way.

Bruce Wayne wasn't afraid to open his doors and share his life with his partners. In the same way, we cannot shut the doors of our lives to one another. We have to fight our battles together, confess when we fail, and help each other up because we know that when we move forward in pursuit of our goal of converting our city, our campus, our high school or our workplace, we can only fail if we don't work together. We must be like Batman who took in the ones who struggled like him, helped them when they fell, and trained them to take on bigger challenges than they ever thought they could face. Because Batman had a vision for them.

What's your vision?

For yourself?

For your friends?

For your world?

We can't be foolish enough to think we can make it on our own. Satan is prowling around like a lion looking for the lone straggler to devour. We can't allow ourselves to be fooled into thinking this is a one man show. Jesus knew his Apostles could spread the message to the world.

What's your role in his plan? It's okay to doubt or not to know. But doubting and not knowing doesn't mean we give up. Most of us spend our whole lives figuring out who we want to be. In your meditation, listen to God and his plan for you. How can he use you? Who does it involve?

Batman vs. Superman

Interestingly enough, one of Batman's closest friends is the one hero who stands at the other spectrum, often times butting heads with the world's greatest detective. This friend is Superman. The World's Finest comics were meant to bring together the world's two greatest superheroes to fight side by side. Superman and Batman. Two heroes. One mission. Sounds like a win/win situation, right?

Often times Batman and Superman don't see eye to eye. Superman has a variety of powers that make him almost godlike to everyone he encounters. He is the hero of Metropolis and often called a "boy scout" by his fellow heroes. He is seen mostly in the daytime, sun shining, American flag waving, and being the nicest guy in town.

Batman is dark, mostly operating at night. He has no powers other than what his pocketbook can afford. Many in Gotham distrust him although they appreciate his effort. Batman comes across often as cold or obsessive at times, making it hard for others to relate to him.

On more than one occasion, Batman and Superman have had to clash against one another, usually because one or the other has been taken control of by a villain or their ideals have given them separate agendas or even one has been given the order to take the other one down.

Through each of these events they still have remained a close pair of friends. Not just in the Justice League but in their private lives. They often joke with one another and test the other's limits, much to the shock of their peers.

Why do they act this way?

Because they know that deep down inside they have the same mission at heart... they want to make the world a better place. They also know that they simply have two different approaches to that same goal. Batman prefers to stalk his criminals at night because he plays on their fears. Superman can take on crime during the day because he has the power to do incredible feats that can save many people at one time.

Some people would argue about who is the better hero. It doesn't take a genius to figure out who I'd be routing for; however, there is a deeper point to be made. Some people are attracted to the Batman type of hero - dark and mysterious, quiet and strong, methodical and structured. What isn't there to like about a Batman kind of hero?

Unless you're into the happy, light, comedic, unbeatable hero. Superman is super. I know it's redundant but hear me out. His strengths outweigh his weaknesses and he fights the good fight with a smile on his face. He can't lose and he flaunts it. He saves people because he loves life and freedom and there isn't anything wrong with that.

Really, what I've been describing to you are two different types of Christians. Both have the same goal but they go about it in two different ways. To some, the message of redemption from our sins carries a much heavier weight than simply having a good life. Some people feel like they are attracted to certain leaders because of their preaching style.

It's like having one preacher who is known for slamming sin from the pulpit in a ten minute message, scaring everyone straight and another who focuses all his messages on forgiveness and grace and humility. Which do you prefer?

There is a defining answer.

Both.

God needs both preachers to get his point across. Just like he needs both types of Christians to reach those that might turn a deaf ear to one or the other. It's really not that difficult to understand.

One teen worker, growing up in the church, working as a paid minister, living in the "better" part of town, lover of sports, and generally accepted by everyone, will have a certain appeal to the teens in any of those categories because he can relate to them.

The other teen worker, converted in his 20's, working two jobs, living in a rougher part of town, interested in video games, comic books, listening to heavier types of music, and a bit more mysterious to the crowd, can have the exact same effect on the teens who relate with these other traits and characteristics.

I bring this up because the second guy is me. The first is the leader of my ministry. You would think that by us being so different we don't talk that much or even attend the same events; however, this is not the case. When we have a disagreement about a decision we talk it through until we both understand where we are going and why. He has my utmost respect and loyalty as much as any teen. Because we have three things in common that trumps all the differences that would normally split us apart in the world -

God,

Jesus,

And the Holy Spirit.

Our mission is the same. And while we may at times joke about our differences and test our limits with one another, we both have an effective role in reaching out to the teens in our ministry. He can reach the kids that I can't relate well with.

I can do the same with the ones that fall into my way of thinking. We work together like Superman and Batman. Two completely separate heroes, two completely separate ways of accomplishing the same goal. Different gifts given to help meet different needs. He is vital to my ministry. I am vital to his. One without the other could hurt the group. Don't believe me?

In the Bible, Paul writes about different gifts given to Christians and why they are so important:

> "Are all apostles? Are all prophets? Are all teachers? Do all work miracles? Do all have gifts of healing? Do all speak in tongues? Do all interpret? But eagerly desire the greater gifts."

This way, no one person has to fight the fight alone but working together makes it all work smoothly. We are given different gifts to benefit our ministries and proclaim the gospel to those who need it the most. If we don't use our gifts and each other, we only set ourselves up for defeat.

When did Batman get his back broken in the comics? It was in 1993 when Bane, a new villain at the time, walked into Wayne Manor and took out his anger on our favorite hero. Alfred at the time was scrounging for someone to call. He ended up going to Tim Drake's house and asked for help. Why didn't he call Superman?

He could have been there before he hung up the phone. It was because Superman had been killed by Doomsday a few months before. There was no Superman. So Batman paid the price. Batman needed Superman. We can't kid ourselves into thinking we don't need every single person in our ministry to help us make it to heaven.

And with that mentality, how can we live without each other?

I challenge you to look at your ministry. Flaws and all. See the different types of people. See the different types of styles and gifts they possess. See their strengths and weaknesses.

Now see their potential.

Do you have a very good relationship with those least like you? Why not? Is it because you have put up walls in your thinking, kidding yourself into believing they won't understand you and help you? Your differences are only outweighed by your faith. Who can they help that you feel you will have only a minimal impact on? Who do you know that could be impacted by someone like them?

Learn to work together and you can overcome any obstacle Satan throws your way. When Satan comes prowling around your ministry looking for someone to devour, he will find only a strong, united ministry, bonded through the Word of God, the cross, and his promises, ready to face any challenge.

Can you have this type of impact on your ministry?

Can you spread this message to your peers?

In the beginning you may just be one person...

But now we're two.

Chapter 6: Batman Versus Bruce Wayne

"I made a promise on the grave of my parents to rid the city of the evil who took their lives. By day I am Bruce Wayne, billionaire philanthropist. At night, criminals, a cowardly and superstitious lot, call me... Batman."[1]

- Bruce Wayne/Batman [f]

<u>Separating the Man from the Myth</u>

I honestly have to admit it. When I used to watch the old school Batman television series, I used to watch Bruce Wayne and think... "Put the costume on! Get back to being Batman! Who cares about Bruce Wayne?"

Most of the movies, shows and comics I saw that had Bruce Wayne in them were a waste of comic page space, in my opinion. Every time Bruce went into public, panic ensued and he had to become Batman again, so why did he bother trying to be a "normal person?"

Did Bruce even like being around bystanders? He always seemed to be hiding things from co-workers, friends, and anyone who tried to get close.

Looking deeper inside the man, I would later realize I was the one being fooled. Just the way Bruce wanted me to. I played right into his hands. I saw Bruce Wayne for a weak individual. Batman was the cool, strong one.

But aren't they one and the same?

Bruce Wayne, the boy, died the same day as his parents. His childhood was dead. His hopes for a normal life were dead. Only one thing survived that night on the cold streets of Crime Alley...

A seed.

For years growing up Bruce Wayne tried to keep a promise. A promise that he would dedicate himself to making the wrong in the world right. A promise to be more than a mere man. He trains his body to near perfection. He focuses his mind to see past what the normal person sees and become the world's greatest detective.

Using the vast wealth of his company, he creates state-of-the-art tools to combat crime. He keeps the world just at arm's length so no one perceives his true motives and he drapes himself in shadow, stalking the vile creatures that plague the city he swore to defend. He will not stop until his pain has been quenched. He is Batman.

In the Darkness, but not of the Darkness

Ultimately, Batman is nothing without Bruce Wayne. There have been more than one person to put on Batman's cowl but all keep coming up short. Bruce Wayne is quite possibly the only one who can be Batman. No one else has the drive, conviction, or perseverance Bruce Wayne has drilled into himself.

In 1993, when Batman had his back broken by Bane during the Knightfall series, the mantle of the bat passed to Jean Paul Valley. Batman readers dubbed him "Azbat," merging Jean Paul's alter ego, Azrael, with Batman. Ruthless and dark, he crossed the line Bruce would not. He would kill those who stood in his way. Removing Robin from the dynamic duo and going solo, readers knew it would only be a matter of time before Bruce Wayne returned and claimed back his birthright.

Even Dick Grayson, both Nightwing and the original Robin, became Batman for a time while Bruce took the time to heal from his wounds from Bane. During that time, Bruce and Dick were able to work out strains in their relationship. Dick may have been a good Batman but he wasn't interested in following in his mentor's path. He had a city of his own to defend and was more than happy to let Bruce return to the cape and cowl.

The insight into Bruce's motivation is what keeps anyone else in the world from becoming the true Batman. No one else seems to understand his pain or sense of justice. Why won't he cross the line of killing a criminal? What if the person really deserved it?

The Joker for one, has put hundreds of people into their graves - more notably, Jason Todd, the second Robin and Commissioner Gordon's wife, Sarah. So when will Batman come to the conclusion that enough is enough?

Never.

That's the whole point of Batman. Journey into the darkness and go where normal people are afraid. Confront evil at its doorstep and catch it off guard. Bring down those who cross the line of evil but never become one of them. Batman walks that line very closely and on more than one occasion has come to the conclusion that he must cross that line to make everything ok. He is always stopped by reason, logic and those closest to him.

During the Hush storyline, the Joker seemingly killed one of Bruce Wayne's oldest friends and Bruce decides the Joker must die to prevent him from causing him any more pain.

The person who reasons with him before he chokes the life from his twisted rival is James Gordon. His wife, having been murdered by the Joker not long before was still fresh on his heart but even he rose to be Batman's conscience. As Batman begins to cross the line, he thinks to himself:

> *"Despite all efforts, I know very little about his origin, who he was before he became the monster he is today.*

(Nightwing) explained to me once that the Joker and I are forever linked in constant battle. That in some way the Joker exists because of me. How I represent the order that is necessary to live in Gotham city and the Joker is the chaos that disrupts that order.

I think about what Nightwing said. My being responsible for the Joker as years worth of rage course through my fist.

I cannot... I will not... accept any responsibility... for the Joker. Except that I should have killed him long ago." [g]

James Gordon stepped in to stop Bruce, not Batman. To lose Batman would mean to lose the man under the mask. If Bruce broke his promise to his parents he would be no better than the man who took their lives.

Everything he worked for would be lost. No one else could get through to Bruce except Jim. If anyone would want to see the Joker dead, surely it was him. He told Batman that he wouldn't let either of them cross the line into evil because they had to be better than that. They had to believe there was a better way and that it worked. Letting go of the Joker, Batman sought comfort from his friend.

Conquering the Darkness Within

What good were Batman's skills and strength if he used them to kill? Anyone could do that. That's not the way of the hero. That's not the way of the Batman. His compassion for human life is what set him apart from the foes he would face. Ultimately, his foes will always have the hope of redemption with Batman.

We as Christians must have the same hope. We allow ourselves to be all things to all men (1Corinthians 9:22), but never cross the line into condemnation. We rely on each other to help us out of sin and into the light while struggling to bring the foes of Christ to peace with Him.

Have you ever met someone who became a Christian though you thought they wouldn't because of where they were at in their life? Isn't the battle for their soul worth it? Don't the hard times and struggles pay off in the end? This is the battle Bruce has every time he brings one of his foes to Blackgate. The hope that they will see the damage they've done to their lives and try to find hope.

Now, whenever I see Bruce Wayne I see more than a weak, bumbling, rich boy, but the mask Batman puts on to fit in with those around him. The true identity is Batman. He lives to make the wrong things right.

He becomes Bruce Wayne to fit in with everyone else. Most people in Gotham don't see Bruce as a hero but they feel they can at least relate to him as a human. However, despite the difference in appearance they are both one person.

Can you imagine if Bruce never became Batman? How different would he be? He might be charitable but he wouldn't have any impact on the crime of his city. If he were always Batman he would miss out on the chance to actually interact with normal people, always being shrouded in darkness.

Batman isn't really that different from Jesus. Jesus is both by nature the God of the universe and yet taking the form of a human servant to show His creation how to be godly.

He never used his powers for himself even to the extent of saving himself from a terrible death. He only used his power for the benefit of others. He made his life a living example of how we should care about those around us.

So too, must our lives be. Not just one way with our friends and family and another way at church. They have to be one and the same. We worship God with our whole heart and become like other men to win as many as possible to the cause. We are the hero God sees in us. People don't always see us for the hero we are or want to be but they can at least relate to us as a human being with struggles and conflicts and the need for repentance and love.

To give us a clearer illustration of this, Paul describes it to his audience when he writes in Philippians 2:1-11:

> *"If you have any encouragement from being united with Christ, if any comfort from his love, if any fellowship with the Spirit, if any tenderness and compassion, then make my joy complete by being like-minded, having the same love, being one in spirit and purpose. Do nothing out of selfish ambition or vain conceit, but in humility consider others better than yourselves. Each of you should look not only to your own interests, but also to the interests of others.*
>
> *Your attitude should be the same as that of Christ Jesus: Who, being in very nature God, did not consider equality with God something to be grasped, but made himself nothing, taking the very nature of a servant, being made in human likeness. And being found in appearance as a man, he humbled himself and became obedient to death— even death on a cross!*
>
> *Therefore God exalted him to the highest place and gave him the name that is above every name, that at the name of Jesus every knee should bow, in heaven and on earth and under the earth, and every tongue confess that Jesus Christ is Lord, to the glory of God the Father."*

I bet you never thought of Jesus as someone with a secret identity before, did you? Think about the pressure that was on him! If he messed up one time, said the wrong thing, acted selfishly just one time... the prophecies about him would be false! He wouldn't be the

Lamb of God anymore and we'd be stuck in our sins forever. The fact that he never gave in even once makes him the ultimate hero. He did it so he could relate to us in our weaknesses.

Who do you relate to? Are there certain types of people you feel more comfortable around and share common interests with? Musicians, skaters, the gothic crowd, preppy kids, the thugs and gangstas, or maybe the extremely religious crowd? Who can you help? When I talk about sharing your faith with the person closest to you, who do you think about? Have you tried to share your faith with that person? Do they even know you're a Christian? What would it take to have a grand impact on their lives? Ultimately... do you want to help them?

Imagine their life changed for God. Don't you think that would impact their families? Their friends? Their neighbors? Don't shelter your godly identity from them. If Bruce didn't become Batman, he definitely wouldn't have helped anyone or had the same impact that he wanted to have on peoples' lives.

In *Batman Begins*, while Bruce is in training, he is confronted by Ducard with the idea that his father was to blame for his parent's death. Bruce counters the argument by saying that he had been trained and that his father was defenseless. What Ducard was saying was that without the will to act, the training is useless. He is right.

In the same way, if we don't step up to the challenge of helping other people we will deny the part of ourselves that could really make a difference in this world. It's all a matter of knowing when and how to act. We just have to be willing.

Chapter 7: The Heart of a Hero

<u>Three Stories of Compassion</u>

We all at times can feel alone. In Bruce Wayne's case, it would be an all-too-familiar feeling. With his parents gunned down in front of him, he caught a glimpse of how cold and cruel the world could really be. The two people that loved Bruce the most were gone forever from his life.

What kept Bruce from turning down the path of a villain? Why didn't he become a monster like the Joker or uncaring like Mr. Freeze? What makes Bruce so different than the foes he faces on a nightly basis?

Love.

Love that started with his parents. A love that continues to flow to the streets of Gotham. Bruce loved his parents very much. They are the sole reason he dons his costume every night for the rest of his life. The love he missed would be the drive for Bruce so that no one else would ever have to suffer the way he did.

Compassion is not a characteristic that one would think of when it comes to Batman. In Batman issue #423, one of my first and favorite issues, three different cops get to share their experiences they've had with Batman.

In the first story, a heroin-addicted man threatens to kill himself by jumping off a bridge. Before he can jump, Batman shows up on the scene. The man rants and raves about how he got the short end of the stick his whole life and that it isn't worth fighting anymore. He can't shake his addiction and he doesn't want to go on.

Leaping off the bridge, Batman jumps after him and grabs him 20 feet above the water. He is secured by a harness and holds the confused man in his grasp. Batman tells him that he has just gotten a second chance at his life and to take advantage of the time he has left. The frightened junkie falls into police custody and is taken to a drug rehabilitation clinic.

In the second story, a group of skinheads took over a grocery store and after taking hostages, decided to kill a few. Batman came crashing in and beat down every one until he got to the last thug. Holding an old woman hostage, the thug said he would kill the woman.

Batman intimidated the thug into pointing the gun at him instead of the woman, which gave Batman the opportunity to attack and subdue him. Everyone was safe in the end and Batman vanished into the night.

The third story was about a little boy and girl who were being chased for stealing food. While they were outrunning the police, they ran into Batman. The police officer was afraid of what Batman would do, but his fears were subsided when he saw Batman talk to the kids and find out what their story was.

It turns out that the children's mother had been killed in a car accident and the father was murdered in a gambling parlor. When the caseworker assigned to them tried to split the two up, they ran away and lived on the streets.

Hearing the story, Batman himself was moved to tears. The police officer was shocked to see the Dark Knight moved in such a way that he actually shed tears for the children. Bruce Wayne would take the children into his home until they were adopted some time later.

These various pictures of Batman show us several different traits that we must also show in our lives if we want to have an impact on this world. For us men, it is not very popular to show emotions like compassion or empathy in public. We are taught that pain is a way of life and crying is for babies. We have to be the strong, emotionless, breadwinners of our family and we don't let anything get us down.

Obviously, this isn't the picture we see of Batman here and it's not the picture we get of Jesus in the Bible. Each of these events reminds me of certain encounters Jesus has with others in the gospels.

In the first story, I am reminded of Jesus' parable of the prodigal son. The son is so distraught at his sinful way of life, after spending his inheritance while his father is still alive, that he is willing to go back to his father's house as a slave. When his father sees him from a great distance, he runs to his son and welcomes him back. The son is a bit taken aback by it and humbled, but the father has forgiven him for squandering his inheritance away.

The son didn't have to come back. He could have accepted his fate and died not knowing his father's great love for him. It is the same in the story of Batman and the junkie. The addict is given a second chance he didn't deserve, just like the prodigal son.

Batman was that chance for the junkie.

But Batman had to leap off the bridge to catch him and give him that chance.

The second story is somewhat like the story of the adulteress caught in the act in John 8. The Pharisees were willing to kill her and trap Jesus at the same time. But knowing their thoughts and attitudes, Jesus turns the argument against them and they leave one by one, leaving the woman unscathed from their attacks.

In the same way that Batman turned the fear of pain on the thug, Jesus turned the fear of punishment of sin against those who accused the woman. Both situations were diffused once the perpetrators realized what they were in for if they had decided to enact their punishment.

Jesus was the chance for the adulteress woman.

But Batman had to scare the thug with the consequences of his actions.

Finally in the third story, I am reminded of the story of the man with leprosy in Matthew 8:1-4. The man is a diseased, lonely and shunned man of society. He has probably not felt the warmth of a human touch in years. Jesus, feeling much compassion for him, got close and touched the man, breaking the mold of the way people had treated him.

Jesus was moved by the man's dilemma and knew that he needed and deserved contact with compassionate people. And in the end, because of Jesus' compassion, the man walked away changed forever.

Batman didn't have to talk to the children. In fact, rounding people up and handing them over to the authorities was a way of life for him. But Batman did what was unexpected by the police officer and probably by the children too. He talked to them and felt compassion for them -- even being moved to tears because of their situation.

He took them in, clothed them, gave them food, and stuck with them until they could get to a home with loving parents and not be separated.

Batman was the chance for the abandoned children.

But Batman had to open his heart, listen to the children's story, and act.

Do you see the recurring theme here? Batman was the chance for each of the people he saved to have a better life. He was in the right place at the right time and did the right thing. We have to be willing to do the same, but first we have to open our eyes, hearts, and mouths to do it.

We feel the compassion for others because God first had compassion on us. In Romans 5:8 it says that while we were still sinners, Christ died for us. That means that we have to be willing to do the same. We have to lay down our lives for the lost to gain their trust and access to their true feelings on where they are.

We see people suffering all around us every day. The masks people wear are the ones that say they have nothing wrong in their lives and that they are happy in their sin. Are you happy when you sin? Are the consequences any less severe just because people try to cope with their sin instead of dealing with it? Then why are they any different from us?

They aren't.

Don't kid yourself into thinking that they are any different from you. We all have the same desires in life and the same emotions that drive us and guide us. That is how Batman is able to take down enemies that are twice as strong and powerful than he is because he knows that deep down inside, his foes are living, emotional beings, that have desires, needs, wants, and hearts. By acknowledging one of these basic needs, Batman is able to determine the best way to either defeat or help his enemies. But he has to be willing to care first.

How much do you care?

Does it bother you to know that there are people hurting in your school, job, or family? Do you feel compassion toward them and really want to make a difference in their life?

We all hit rock bottom in our lives at some point in time. The question is, will we face the truth about ourselves and move forward stronger or let ourselves be taken in by our sorrows, pain, and problems? If we possess the will to act, we can and will make a difference in the world around us.

We shouldn't act in a way that will selfishly benefit ourselves. Many people in the world, and in Jesus' day, the Pharisees, gave to the poor with trumpets and much emphasis on themselves. The rich in today's society will give out of their overflow. But when someone helps out of their desire to please God, it brings glory to our Father in heaven.

Jesus talks so much about the poor and meeting people's needs. There are unlimited ways we can help people less fortunate than ourselves. Whether giving financially to individuals, helping out at local shelters or starting a food drive, the possibilities are endless as to how we can take a stand and help those we feel compassion for.

Do we want to keep living our lives as though nothing is wrong with the world around us? It is difficult to open our eyes to the pain of the world because it is overwhelmingly sad to see how others hurt themselves and distance themselves from God, their only true hope. As painful as it is to watch, sometimes it is even more difficult to actually stand up and do what we know is right.

It's easier to turn away when we see someone get picked on for being different. It's simple to walk past the homeless man and think that he will be that way forever. It's not even hard to hate someone because they did something mean to you. If doing the right thing was easy, everyone would be doing it. But it's not easy. It's always an uphill battle, a struggle to challenge us to be different because we want to be different... because we're called to be different.

Helping someone change a character sin in one's life takes time. To develop something into a habit can take weeks or months. Staying in there with each other can take a lot out of you and provide many opportunities to struggle, turn back, and fail. Giving up cannot be an option or eventually it will be your only option.

Did you know that most homeless people don't stay homeless? Most will get back on their feet again but there are others who will take their place. Did you know that after you graduate from high school, no one cares about popularity, even in college?

Did you know that your worst enemy in your mind, is a human just like you and cares about the people closest to him or her? The only hierarchies in this world are the ones we create in our minds. If we want to help people, we have to be able to push past this way of thinking and think like Jesus would.

If knowledge is power, then you've just been given power. By knowing these things we can see the hope past the cloud of smoke that doesn't matter in the long run. We can help people who will change their lives for the better. Who cares if the popular kids at school are the ones thinking they are better than everyone else?

In a few years, reality will have some surprises waiting for them. Who cares if the homeless person uses the money given to him in a way you'd prefer? Isn't God looking for the compassion in our hearts? The question we have to ask ourselves is: What's important **now?**

If we can answer that question on a daily basis we can actively change the world around us and know that what we stand for is the way of the true hero. Not because we have to be or we were told to be, but because we choose to be.

We were meant to be.

But we have to take that chance.

Like Batman, like Jesus, we have to **be** that chance.

Foreword: The Rogues Gallery

There's a common quote, "A hero is defined by his villains." When looking at Batman and his vast array of psychopathic foes, we can begin to understand a lot about Batman.

What makes him so different than the criminals he hunts? Are these villains just chaotic examples of fate or is there more to their madness than we realize? Is it possible that these super-villains can be just as human as you or I? How do we avoid becoming like them?

I'd like to take you on a journey through Arkham Asylum (Blackgate for all you newer readers). Let's examine some of Batman's most heinous foes and determine where they went wrong so we don't make the same mistake they do.

Most of them have fallen into tragic situations that they can't pull themselves out of. Looking at their stories and a few of my own, perhaps I can shed some light on their mentality. They aren't as complex as you might think and we can fall into the same traps if we aren't looking at where we're going.

It's hard to imagine that we have anything in common with the Joker, Clayface, Bane, or even Mr. Freeze. But looking deep into their psyche we can follow their mindset and start to help other people from going down that same path and maybe stop ourselves from doing the same things.

Welcome to the dark side of Gotham. Come... meet the opposition.

Chapter 8: Mr. Freeze – Apathy

"Congratulations... you actually succeeded in making me angry."

Mr. Freeze – *"Batman – Under the Hood"* [h]

Cold From the Beginning

Victor Fries was a small child when he learned about the process of freezing objects. Starting with water and other liquids, Victor discovered there wasn't anything he couldn't freeze. Curiosity made him experiment on insects, plants, and eventually animals. He became fascinated about the process of preserving the world around him.

His curiosity eventually got the best of him. He later dedicated his whole room to frozen artifacts. His vast collection caught the attention of his father. Horrified by Victor's obsession, he destroyed his frozen collection in a fit of rage and condemned Victor to a boarding school, where he could learn to fit in with his peers.

Attending the strict boarding school, Victor was watched around the clock. He had abandoned his collection of frozen artifacts but continued to study the field of cryogenics. He was sure the human body could be preserved beyond death and later be revived. Victor's discoveries helped advance cryogenics beyond what anyone could have hoped.

His success brought him many degrees and friends. One such acquaintance was a girl named Nora. Victor and Nora became great friends as she challenged him on an intellectual level as well as emotional. Over time, the two fell in love and got married.

Victor's life took a terrible twist though, when his beloved Nora fell victim to a terrible disease. Incurable, she eventually died and became cryogenically frozen until medicine could find a cure for her disease. Victor's obsession began anew.

He began working for a company run by a man named Ferris Boyle. He went to work in the cryogenics facilities, frantically studying medicine to help his beloved Nora. He didn't like the work he was in but it helped him pay the bills and raise money for his research.

It was only a matter of time before Victor ran out of money. The cryo-stasis was too expensive to keep up. Ferris demanded that Victor's wife be brought out, ending her life but Victor couldn't let that happen.

Victor confronted Ferris on the matter and after an extensive argument, got violent. Ferris was stronger than Victor and knocked him into a station of chemicals and equipment where he appeared dead. Ferris left him in a panic and got away leaving Victor for dead.

But Victor was not dead. The chemicals and solvents worked into his DNA and caused his body temperature to lower dramatically. Victor awoke to find his skin very cold to the touch and sensitive to heat. Loading his wife's cryo-stasis tube onto a delivery truck, he left to a nearby abandoned meat storage facility where he could pull himself together.

Victor had to stay in sub-zero temperatures to survive. He would later find the materials to create a suit that would conform to his frigid disposition. Even though Victor Fries was now a walking abomination, his first duty was to his wife. He needed to find the money and materials to restore her to life.

He later created a gun that could freeze anything he shot into a block of ice. Taking the name Mr. Freeze, Victor began robbing banks and stealing money that would help him gain supplies from the black markets to help him cure his wife's disease and eventually his own. There was just one thing that kept standing in his way... Batman.

Batman found out about his wife's condition and continued to stop Mr. Freeze in the hope that he would let his company, Wayne Enterprises, help her. Victor refused, thinking he was the only one who could save her. With his wife tucked away in a secret location, no one could get to her.

Eventually, Batman did find the location of Nora Fries and had her moved to Wayne Enterprises cryogenics facilities where Victor's research was used to actually cure her and restore her to life. Victor's fate though, would be much more devastating.

Victor's condition was irreversible and on top of that, he had to serve his sentence for the crimes he committed. Victor's rage at the world seemed to know no bounds. He couldn't even be in the same room as his wife because the room temperature would kill him. Nora tried to calm her husband's rage but failed many times. Seeing the monster Victor had become, Nora divorced Victor and eventually remarried.

Victor Fries shut down emotionally. No one would ever hurt him again. His icy demeanor became his only quality socially. He would never allow anyone to get close or influence him in any way. His hatred inside for what he truly loved, turned toward what anyone in his path loved instead. Victor escaped from Arkham and began a crime spree not motivated by his passion, but others'.

Destroying people's life accomplishments was his first and only mission. If his victim cherished a piece of art, he would destroy it. If it was around a person, he would murder them. He even eventually attacked Bruce Wayne, attempting to kill Alfred because he was his surrogate father, thinking that Bruce looked to him for comfort after his parents died.

Even through Freeze's many defeats, he remains at large to this day, plotting his next move to destroy the objects of other's affections. Victor Fries was frozen deep inside the monster he became... never to return again.

Cold to the Touch

Mr. Freeze's problem is not his anger, although it did spark him to become what he is today. His problem is not that deep. It resides in apathy. He freezes everything in his path to get even with a harsh and cruel world that he blames for his condition.

Freeze does not feel anything emotionally. If someone were to get mugged right in front of him, he wouldn't bother lifting a finger. He can't allow himself to get involved emotionally with anything he comes into contact with. To love would mean he would have to lose it later.

Is there anything in your life that you cling to emotionally? What is the one thing you cherish the most? If there was a fire in your home and you could only save one thing, what would it be? And what would happen if you lost only that one thing?

How would you feel?

How would you cope with the loss? What if it couldn't be replaced? Would we be tempted to be angry at God and the world? We can become so emotionally attached with someone or something that when we lose it, we become so cold to the world around us because we feel like they don't care about us or our loss.

I actually remember at my grandmother's funeral, being mad that the world actually kept going on. That time wouldn't stop so that I could keep the memory of my grandmother alive and fresh forever.

Time would heal my wounds, but at the time I didn't want it to heal. Victor's anger is the same. Why did the world have to keep going for everyone else? Why couldn't it just be frozen and unchanging, so he didn't have to lose any more of his heart?

Victor gave up his emotions as a defense against the cold of the world. Do you know anyone who has shut down emotionally because of what they might have lost? What do they act like? Are they depressed, or confused, or both? What can break through their cold heart?

Issues like feelings of rejection, death, frustration, loss and sin, can harden our hearts. What can break through to the problem and soften us so we don't become like Victor?

I'd like to share a personal example. When I first became the leader of our campus ministry, I had it all together. I had my "to do" list and could knock it out every day. I could invite a hundred people to church and ace my Bible class tests with my eyes closed.

Everyone else in my ministry, you ask?

That was a different story.

People were struggling. I wasn't a bad leader, they were just bad followers. Why couldn't they take my lead? It wasn't my fault. We all had to be responsible for ourselves and our salvation. Doesn't the Bible say work out your own salvation with fear and trembling? (Philippians 2:12)

It was about six months before I was replaced as leader, asked to "co-lead" in a situation that I felt was unfair and as a result, I shut down. Emotionally and spiritually I took a backseat. I chose not to do anything just so I could see the less experienced leader fall on his face. Then they would see the bad decision he had made. When my leader asked for help, I coldly ignored him.

During a very hard stretch, I saw many people in my ministry stop following God. No one stopped coming to church when I was leader. It wouldn't be long before I got my revenge on an ignorant leader who treated me unfairly.

Late one night, I was talking to a brother who was my roommate at the time and we talked about what I was feeling. I expressed the angry feelings I was dealing with (or not dealing with …). I really feel God spoke through him to break my hardened heart.

It wasn't my weak leader's fault that the ministry began to crumble but rather my ignoring them for so long that I wasn't helping anyone. I was apathetic to their needs. When they struggled, I wondered why they didn't keep up instead of helping them along the way. I had a lot of repenting to do.

Confronting my co-leader, I was shocked by how understanding he was with my dilemma. He confessed having the same feelings toward me when I got the leadership position.

I realized then that I didn't deserve the position I had. Maybe one day, but first I had to start helping people again. It couldn't be about the position but about the serving. God had to break my heart to make it soft again.

Thawing Our Own Hearts

Do you have a hard heart towards a brother? What about towards leadership? What about the world? The Bible says we must become like all men to win as many as possible. (1Corinthians 9:21) How can we do that if we don't feel sympathy for them?

Can you imagine what Jesus would have been like if he was apathetic to people's needs? Let's take the woman at the well, in John chapter 4. He could have gotten his own water and let the girl go about her way. He knew she had many struggles with rejection, being married 5 times and being a Samaritan, not just a woman, she shouldn't even be talking to Jesus.

But he made the first move and helped change not just her life, but the lives of everyone in her town. All because Jesus wasn't apathetic to one person's needs.

Can we be the same? Can't we reach out to those we feel will probably reject us? Of course we can. Often times I find it is those who I think are less open to be the most open of anyone I meet. God does that to shame our wisdom and futile thinking.

It's okay though, I enjoy the surprises.

Mr. Freeze couldn't let himself feel anything towards the world because he refused to be hurt again. We can get that way sometimes too, wishing God would just wrap this thing up and end it all. If we don't put ourselves out there, vulnerable and willing, we can keep pretending that if it's "out of sight, it's out of mind." Then we let people walk out of our lives and ultimately out of hope.

We have so much to share.

Why are we so closed to people's needs?

It's our empathy, not our apathy that will help us from becoming like Mr. Freeze. Listening to people who are hurting will help us when we are hurting; to be open and confrontational with our sin, keeping us from hardening our hearts toward God, his people and the world around us.

Chapter 9: Two-Face – Hypocrisy and Duality

"Fate has cursed me with duality and I decided long ago that it is my ugly evil side which dominates! Similarly Batman's fate --given destiny is to oppose evil and ugliness. I act and he reacts! Let him come!"

-Two Face – Batman #397 [i]

The Duality of Harvey Dent

The first comic of Batman I ever received was Batman #397, and it involved Two-Face. Ever since then, he has been my favorite Batman villain. I even created a Two-Face suit for Halloween. One year I also bought a Two-Face action figure so that I could get a coin that was like the one he had in the comics. Beyond that, I guess I just thought a villain with the struggle of being a hero all wrapped up in one was too cool to pass up.

To fall into Two-Face's hands would have been a terrifying thing. Working for him would be just as bad. On the bright side, his victims always had a fifty-fifty chance to live. If the coin landed scarred side up, though, there would be no negotiating. You were toast.

To understand Two-Face's mindset, you have to go back to the beginning of Batman's story. When Batman and Commissioner Gordon first teamed together, catching the bad guys wasn't that difficult. Keeping them locked up, though, was.

Criminals had a knack for buying off the cops, lawyers, and judges to gain freedom. Batman and Gordon needed someone they could trust to never fold on his convictions. Harvey Dent rose to the occasion.

Batman would take down the lawless, Gordon would make the arrest, and Dent would keep them behind bars. After catching a good number of crime bosses, they were close to catching the head crime boss of the city... Salvatore "The Boss" Maroni. After Batman and Gordon made their move, Maroni was finally behind bars. All they needed was Dent to make the final move.

In the middle of the hearing, Dent was introducing as evidence Maroni's lucky trinket, a double-headed Gotham mint coin, which linked him to the crime. As Dent went to make his closing remarks, Maroni threw acid in Dent's face, scarring the left half of his head. Dent was rushed to the hospital, but the acid that scarred Dent's face ran deeper on his psyche than anyone realized. Maroni had no idea the demon he had unleashed.

Harvey Dent's past was a lot darker than the bright courageous persona he upheld in the public light. Before he became a district attorney, Dent had a hard life. He harbored much anger and was picked on when he was in school. One day, when a bully pushed Dent too far, he attacked the child and put him in the hospital, nearly killing him. Dent felt so bad that he began to bury his anger deep within himself, vowing to never release it again.

Maroni's act of cruelty opened the twisted door within Dent's soul and unleashed his anger, in the form of another personality, the personality that would be known as Two-Face, the most feared crime boss in all of Gotham.

Harvey, overwhelmed with anger and confusion, fled the hospital and using his knowledge of crime, hired thugs and bodyguards while he plotted his revenge. Obsessed with the irony of his new disposition, he took Maroni's lucky coin and scarred one side to match his twisted persona. He even created his suits to match his face, one side usually being very nice material, the other half, very ugly material. Blaming luck and chance for his new birth, he would use the same "luck," to decide the outcomes of all his crimes. When the opportunity would present itself, he would flip the coin, and depending on the side it landed on, he would follow its ruling to whatever end.

One example is while robbing a bank, one of Two-Face's men went to steal a wedding ring from a teller, Two-Face stopped and flipped the coin. It landed clean heads up and he demanded the ring be returned.

Harvey would battle with being good and evil over and over again in every crime he went to commit. Soon he would try and have his crimes dictated by the number two, stealing in multiples of two, at times usually at two in the morning or afternoon. Sometimes he would have two crimes committed at once, throwing Batman off.

Once, during the "No Man's Land" stories, Harvey caught commissioner Gordon and put him on trial. Two-Face was the judge and the prosecutor. In the end, however, Dent's personality came forth and rebutted Two-Face's arguments and put forth such a case that he actually had Gordon acquitted and set free. In Two-Face's comic appearances, it was considered to be one of his best stories.

Two-Face has more than one problem in his life. Looking at the character of Two-Face, we can learn a lot about how we should be (and not be) in our Christian walk.

The story of Two-Face reminds me of the scripture in James 4:15-17. It reads :

> "Instead, you ought to say, "If it is the Lord's will, we will live and do this or that." As it is, you boast and brag. All such boasting is evil. Anyone, then, who knows the good he ought to do and doesn't do it, sins."

Harvey knows the good he ought to do. He just leaves it up to fate to determine what he does. He ignores his conscience, and follows through on whatever path his coin lays out for him, to the bitter or happy end. When Harvey's coin comes clean side up, he can be a veritable force for good. He was a good law keeper, but when his coin side comes scarred side up, all he is, is a hypocrite.

Harvey's belief in luck and face of the coin determine his motivation. One of Two-Face's greatest strengths is his knowledge of the law. The Pharisees and Sadducees knew the law like the back of their hand. For whatever reason, they chose to enforce it, but not follow it. Jesus' seven woes give us an idea of what their hearts and minds were like. Here is a good passage to reflect upon:

> "Woe to you, teachers of the law and Pharisees, you hypocrites! You are like whitewashed tombs, which look beautiful on the outside but on the inside are full of dead men's bones and everything unclean. In the same way, on the outside you appear to people as righteous but on the inside you are full of hypocrisy and wickedness."
> (Matthew 23:27-28)

Physically, Harvey was the definition of handsome. His nickname was Harvey "Apollo" Dent. Inside, however, he was as dark as night -- the exact opposite of what everyone, even his good friend Bruce Wayne, thought. Outside he appeared as righteous, but inside, Two-Face was evil.

Batman Versus Two-Face

Batman has to watch the line he walks every night. One slip or action with a wrong motive, and he becomes a villain, just like Two-Face. In Frank Miller's "The Dark Night Returns," Batman's first fight from ten years of retirement is the battle with a healed Harvey Dent. Harvey's face was fixed through surgery, but the toll had been too much. Two-Face was all that remained. When Batman finally defeated Harvey, he pulled the bandages off and saw that Harvey's face was fine. In Harvey's mind, however, all hope was lost. Asking

Batman what he saw, all he could say was a reflection. Harvey would not escape his demons; neither would Bruce.

This does not mean that we give up on those who confess to be Christians, but don't live the life or fall into sin. In fact, we make it our mission to show our friends the right way to do things to encourage repentance from sin. If they don't see the right way to do things, how can they hope to change?

That's why we must be on guard not to become hypocritical. Does this mean we're perfect? No. Not by a long shot, and we still get the chance to repent, as long as we don't bury the good side of ourselves and let sin continue, like Two-Face does. In 1Timothy 4:16, the Bible says "Watch your life and doctrine closely, persevere in them. For if you do, you will save both yourself and your hearers."

People are watching, waiting to call us hypocritical or liars to our face. Such people are shallow and forgetful of their own shortcomings, but we must fight this mentality. We will save our hearers if we hold to what we are taught by Jesus and his words in the Bible. We just have to persevere.

Do you know many people who have walked away from the faith and returned to their previous lives before Christ? What do they act like? Is it the happy experience they thought it would be, or are there aspects of their lives that warn us to stay away and deny sin? Do you see the correlation with Harvey Dent?

Two-Face's blatant refusal to follow the law is in mockery to what his life was all about, and it has destroyed many people's lives because of his refusal to do the right thing or get help. No one can make the choice for him. Not Batman, not Gordon. Only Harvey can make the decision to turn himself in.

Does this mean we give up on those who have made the decision to leave God? No. We continue to be the example for them, just like Batman. He never resorts to calling Harvey by his criminal name, Two-Face. He always calls him Harvey, because he has faith he will reach his long lost friend. So too it is with us. We don't give up on anyone until death takes their last chance from this world.

To battle our darker halves, we must be willing to confront it. If we lie to ourselves, we only give strength to the side we want to fight. But if we are honest with ourselves, get open with other people when we struggle, or get humble when we are confronted with a sin, we conquer the dark side of ourselves that wishes to see us fail.

Closing ourselves off from God's word is much like letting Satan flip the coin of salvation or condemnation in our lives… it is only a matter of time before the wrong side comes up.

Chapter 10: Clayface – Addiction

The Cost of Fame

There once was a famous actor in Gotham named Matt Hagen. The roles he played won him various awards recognizing his acting skills and charisma. A few more major roles and Matt would be set for life.

Unfortunately for Matt, those roles would never come. Late one night Matt was in a horrendous car accident. His face was smashed into a thousand pieces. It didn't take Matt's agent long to determine he would never be able to work the same roles he had previously done. He would be transformed into a voice actor at best.

Depressed and suicidal, Matt thought his career was over. That is until one night, a man named Roland Daggett showed up. Roland had an answer for Matt's depression. It was a facial cream called Renew-U. Putting the cream on his face, Matt could mold his face to whatever he desired... even like it was before his accident.

Matt quickly returned to the acting circuit under the guise that he had been repaired with a new plastic surgery. His roles were better than ever, and he kept on trying to live his dream. It didn't take long though, until Matt realized there was something wrong with Renew-U.

Returning to Roland Daggett, Matt discovered that the mysterious substance he had been using to reshape his face contained addictive properties that made it almost painful to be without. Using Matt's addiction to his advantage, Roland kept raising the price on the Renew-U Matt needed until he could no longer afford it. Roland then suggested to Matt that he use the cream to impersonate other people and commit crimes to gain more money.

Doing just that, he even one time impersonated Bruce Wayne to steal money from Wayne Enterprises.

This of course, gained Batman's attention and the Dark Knight went out to investigate.

After choosing to never commit crimes again for Daggett, Matt broke into Roland's factories and tried to steal a large portion of the Renew-U, expose Roland's evil plots and be rid of Daggett once and for all. However, Matt got caught by Daggett's men and they forced him to ingest a concentrated large amount of the drug and left him for dead.

Matt awoke later and feeling sick, he went home to work out what had happened. His best friend was there and while Matt was looking at his awards for his various roles, his face began to switch to the characters he had played in the past. He then realized he could at will, change his body and appearance to mimic nearly anything he chose, living or not. Realizing his new powers, he made a plan to enact his revenge on Daggett.

Roland Daggett appeared on a local talk show in an attempt to gain support for Renew-U which he planned to sell on the main market to anyone who wanted to look different. It was then that a woman stood up and confronted Daggett on the addictive properties and pain it caused anyone who used the product. Daggett tried to deny the charges, but then the woman changed into Matt's new form and he showed the world what he now was -- the abomination known as Clayface.

Clayface's attempt on Daggett's life was thwarted by Batman, but Clayface escaped the police by faking his own death. To this day, Clayface remains one of Batman's most deadly enemies because Batman knows he could walk by him at any time and not realize it was him.

Venom and Renew-U

Clayface is not the only character in Batman's world to face addiction. In fact a number of villains use drugs on their victims often times leading to the person having to seek medical help to bring their lives back to normal.

Another villain Batman faces that has had to deal with addiction is Bane. Bane's size and strength was derived from a serum called Venom. It gave its user a boost of adrenaline and strength but left behind a strong urge to become violent as well.

In the storyline, *Batman: Venom*, Bruce witnesses a little girl's death when he was powerless to stop it. Batman then began taking the drug called Venom to ensure that he would never be weak again. Realizing his mistake and undergoing serious withdrawal, he had to eventually overcome his addiction, almost costing him his life. Because of this, he knew the powerful threat Bane could really be.

The main positive that came from the Venom experience, was that by Bruce, while overcoming his addiction, gained the experience he needs to help others who are addicted to drugs.

Bane's first major battle with Batman showed his dependence on the toxin. Even after breaking Batman's back, Bane had to face a new Batman who exploited his need for the drug and caused him to go into a craving fit, which ultimately brought the villain down.

Over some time, Bane managed to beat his addiction to the drug, relying on his own strength to try and bring Batman down. While his popularity has dwindled a bit over time, Bane will always be remembered for his addiction to the toxin that almost claimed his life.

It is the same with Clayface. Deep down inside is the mind of Matt Hagen, Gotham superstar. Outside, through Clayface, Matt's addiction has taken over. Matt has ultimately become his addiction. His craving for Renew-U made him resort to doing things Matt Hagen would never do.

In this, we must remember that addiction is very powerful. Nicotine, caffeine, and alcohol are the three easiest addictions to succumb to in America because they are all legal. What happens when someone goes without a cigarette for a day, or a coke, or a drink to take the edge off?

If the withdrawal causes them to fall into sin, whether it is anger, frustration or irritability, then there may be a tougher issue to deal with inside the person's mind. Being around someone who is trying to quit any of these substances can be somewhat difficult. Bad attitudes and frustration quickly take the place of a usually quiet demeanor.

The illegal drugs are more costly for body and mind. One dose of meth, heroine, crack, and cocaine can kill a person. Even LSD can cause brain damage if too much is taken at one time.

Matt Hagen could have easily died that night he was forced to drink the vat of Renew-U. But he didn't. His body succumbed to the toxins and took control of Matt's life. He didn't even try to get help for his condition and as long as that remains his choice, he will never become Matt Hagen again.

The actor once loved by countless masses is truly dead inside. If Batman could help Matt understand his perspective of addiction, perhaps Matt could overcome and change.

Addiction and the Soul

Addiction is by far one of the most dangerous and costly sins one might face in America today. Addiction tears apart families, cost large amounts of money, and leads to sins of all kinds.

People can be addicted to many things, not just drugs. People can be addicted to sex, pornography, alcohol, money, attention, food, and countless other things. They exist because deep down inside the addict, there is a huge gaping hole that they think they can fill with something that makes them happy or makes them not have to think about their struggles.

Often times I've heard preachers refer to this as a "God-shaped hole." People who become addicted to drugs don't start out that way. They experiment first. They use the drugs as a tool to make them forget their pain.

A high created by marijuana, cocaine, LSD, ecstasy, or speed, can make the person feel like they are on top of the world or immune to the consequences of the decisions they've made in their lives. The only problem is that when the "high" is over, the problems are still there waiting for them.

The problems soon become the least of a person's worries when he or she becomes addicted to the drug. Some drugs become very expensive as the addict's body builds a tolerance against the high, requiring greater amounts to maintain not just the high effect but just to feel normal.

A good friend and brother of mine at church spoke to me about some of the troubles he faced before finding Christ. "When you're an addict, you'll do anything to get the money you need.

I had a $1,500-a-day addiction, and I had almost no trouble getting the money. I would go out and lie to people all the time and gain their sympathy to get what I needed. I didn't care who it came from, just as long as I got the money."

This brother leads a C.R. (Chemical Recovery) ministry in our church. It is a bit of a tough love program designed specifically to help people who want to be Christians kick their habits and recover their normal lives while walking with God all the way. Many brothers and sisters in the faith have pulled through such hard times to be where they are today... clean, sober, and praising God.

Sometimes to help someone trapped in addiction, we have to first understand what they are going through. There are many books written and designed to help people not just overcome their addiction but to find God in the process.

Sometimes we have to wait until the person hits rock bottom before they will truly seek the help you can give. In many group-enabled therapy sessions, the addict cannot be helped until he or she first admits that he or she has a problem. It can be difficult for an addict to take this first step and admit that there is a problem but once they do, their path to recovery can be one filled with hope.

If you'd like to help someone who is struggling with addiction, there are a number of drug rehabilitation clinics in any given city. Speak to your pastor and see what they can offer in the form of support and experience. You may find that you truly have what it takes to help people who feel like they have no hope.

The Battle for those Consumed

In this fight of ours, we must not consider those wrapped in their addiction as the enemy. Satan is our enemy and he is using people's weaknesses against them. To overcome him physically, we have to overcome him mentally and spiritually.

There are several stories and examples the Bible gives us when dealing with drugs. In Galatians 5:19-21, Paul tells us that witchcraft and drunkenness will keep us from inheriting the kingdom of God. Witchcraft was defined as using substances to alter your state of mind. It was not uncommon for those practicing witchcraft to do so in rituals of revenge and incantation of pagan spirits. Addiction to such substances would not be addressed for many centuries later.

Many people wanting to rationalize their abuse of such drugs as marijuana and alcohol say that there is nothing wrong with their inebriation. Peter also addresses disciples who were struggling with alcohol consumption in 1 Peter 4:7, when he says:

"Therefore be clear minded and self-controlled so that you can pray."

So you see that we have to stay in our right minds because we know that prayer is powerful. The Bible says again that the prayers of a righteous man are powerful and effective citing that Elijah, a man like us, prayed once and God withheld rain from Israel for three years, and with another, opened the skies again. (James 5:15-17)

In both testaments, when people drank too much, bad things happened. When Noah got drunk, one of his three sons ended up being cursed. When Lot got drunk, he committed incest with his two daughters.

When Sampson got drunk, he gave away the source of his strength to his enemies, which ended in his own death. Paul told the Corinthian church that their meetings did more harm than good because people were getting drunk while taking communion! (1 Corinthians 11:17)

There are individuals in this world that are trying to push for the legalization of drugs. I've even heard a liberal radio talk-show trying to make people who are against drug legalization out to be fools.

What they fail to see is that such laws would create uncontrolled abuse of very dangerous drugs and desperation to get those drugs. Clinics would be flooded with people trying to kick their addictions. People would be racing to take those drugs and make them more potent and intoxicating. We must stand against those who would cast that type of shadow over our society.

If Daggett had gotten his drug into the public's hands, he would have created a society that would have paid a heavy price for the gift of beauty. We must be like Batman and help those who have fallen into the traps of such men as Daggett before they become the soul torn shadows of themselves, like Clayface.

Chapter 11: Wrath – Anger and Vengeance

The Player on the Other Side

On June 26th, a boy stood in terror as his father and mother were gunned down on the streets of Gotham. The boy dedicated his life to fighting people like those who killed his parents. After training his body and mind to their peak, the boy took to the night and struck hard against all who stood in his way.

If you think I'm writing about Bruce Wayne... you're wrong. I'm writing about the character known as Wrath, a virtually unknown villain in the DC universe. The story title of Wrath's only appearance was called "The Player on the Other Side."

First appearing in Batman Special No. 1 in 1984, it would also be Wrath's last appearance. His story mirrored that of Bruce Wayne almost exactly. He even donned a costume that many mistook for Batman. The main difference is that Wrath's parents were criminals and their killer was the officer James Gordon.

Armed with an arsenal of weapons and the same dedication toward his enemies only Batman shares, Wrath grew up killing officers until he could get to Gordon.

Wrath accomplished a lot during his short comic appearance. He discovered Batman's identity, vandalized Bruce's parents tombstone, attempted three assassination plots on Commissioner Gordon, and hospitalized Batman's butler, Alfred. Through the entire endeavor, Batman and Gordon never knew who Wrath was or why he hated them so much. He seemed to match Batman's prowess, agility, focus, and strengths in every way. His life of vengeance and hatred were about to reap their just consequences.

In the end, Batman would face Wrath on a rooftop just above where Bruce's parents were killed. Thinking he had killed Commissioner Gordon, Wrath began preparations to kill Batman next. Once realizing Gordon's wounds were faked, he flew into a rage and in a struggle with Batman, set the rooftop they were on ablaze.

After Wrath gained the upper hand, stabbing Batman, the tides were turned and Batman threw him over his shoulder accidentally into the fire. Wrath stumbled to the ledge of the building and fell to his death, stories below.

The Wrath of the Batman

Wrath, short-lived as his story was, was still one of the most powerful stories I had read. An evil Batman would be hard to stop, mainly because of the obsession they both seem to possess. But perhaps there is something to be learned in this one issue. Something bigger.

You see, although he mirrored Batman in almost every way, he crossed the line Batman would not.

He killed for vengeance.

Batman knows that if he were to kill someone out of anger, he could never come back to the way he was. Wrath never considered anything else. It would be easy for Batman to strike at the heart of criminality and destroy his foes. It would be easier to end his problems than deal with them. Who in Gotham could compare to his agility, determination and loss? No one... but Wrath.

Even in his name, Wrath stirs up a variety of emotions and thoughts. Wrath isn't the same as anger. Wrath is backed up with action. Wrath is vindictive, unreasoning, and malicious. Wrath would not let his enemies escape his anger. Anyone who got in his way would pay the ultimate price.

Batman would be no different if he did the same to criminals. In *Batman Begins*, Bruce Wayne must make a decision. Kill a murderer and administer justice or spare him and forfeit his life.

Bruce tried to explain to Ra's al Ghul that his compassion for life was important because it separated him from the criminals. In this he makes his first stand as a hero: He will not kill. Ever.

If he allowed himself to take someone's life, he would make himself no better than the man who murdered his parents. In Bruce's mind, this is simply not an option. Once he makes his stand, he miraculously escapes the League of Shadow compound unscathed.

When he made the right decision, someone was watching out for him.

Conquering the Wrath in our Lives

In my own life I struggled with anger immensely. I would lose my temper whenever something didn't go my way, when someone would pass me wrong on the highway, when someone said something I didn't like... it didn't stop.

It consumed me at every turn. I had read several times Genesis 4:6 when God told Cain, "...*sin is crouching at your door; it desires to have you, but you must master it.*" But it was so difficult. I even held a grudge against my roommate Sean for over a year, simply because we both liked the same girl. One night, when we both realized we couldn't take it anymore, we talked it through. Once I realized what I was doing, it hit me like a ton of bricks.

I always had to have a villain in my life.

I would project my anger onto something because it simply gave me a reason to be mad. It gave me something to fight. I longed for the battles I would fight over and over again in my mind. I would have fifty ways to get back at someone who I had just met... and they hadn't done anything to me!

I had to let my anger go or it would destroy my life and everything I held dear! I had been backstabbed by one too many people and I wasn't ready to trust anyone. As soon as I realized what I was doing, it scared me. How could I do this to the people I cared about? Once I faced this fact, only then could I change and let trust back into my relationships.

Eventually, I had to find a scripture to help me in my daily efforts to overcome my anger and frustration. Every time I would get the feeling of becoming uncontrollably upset, I would quote my favorite scripture to myself. *"Do not let your hearts be troubled. Trust in God. Trust also in me."* (Jesus – John 14:1) Saying this to myself made me lean on God and trust that if he were in control, things would work out.

Perhaps I just needed the patience to wait and see why my circumstances were working out the way they did. I can't tell you how often things resolved themselves in the most unexpected ways. Sometimes I got myself under control, sometimes not. My failures taught me a great deal about patience and self-control. My victories brought about a changed heart and mindset. I would see the fruits of my patience, even to this day.

My roommate and I did finally patch up our relationship and can openly joke about it today. Not that it was a laughing matter at the time, but we see how silly I was to cling to such animosity. I try to trust people more in my life and honestly I haven't looked back. I truly understand that if in my life I have been wronged, that God will repay. (Romans 12:19) I leave it to God to avenge.

Wrath could not make this kind of decision. He projected his hate onto any police officer he laid his eyes on. His anger and wrath were his only relief and it drove him ultimately, into his grave. That's the difference between Batman and Wrath.

Batman is willing to put his faith in the system and not avenge himself or his parents in the same way they were killed. Batman was willing to hold to his convictions. Wrath was destroyed by them. In the end it was the only fate for Wrath. For Jesus said, *"Those who live by the sword, die by the sword."* (Matthew 26:52) In other words, those who live by wrath will die in wrath.

Do you struggle with anger? How easy is it for you to lose your temper?

Who do you get angry at the most? How can you remedy the wounds?

If you struggle with anger, don't let it get the best of you. Make restitution and peace with yourself and whoever you're mad at. Be open. Don't let Satan get a foothold on you and your relationships. Remember he's looking for every opportunity to get you alone and take you down. You're stronger than that, and now you know his schemes.

Don't be like Wrath. Your compassion is a strength. That's why it's so important. It's what separates you from the soldiers of darkness.

You have the choice to do great or terrible things, and I have faith in you.

Chapter 12: The Red Hood – Guilt and Forgiveness

"I've always wondered... always... was he scared at the end? Was he praying I'd come save him? And in those last moments when he knew that I wouldn't... did he hate me for it?"

-Batman (Batman issue 641) [j]

The Torment of Guilt

How many times did Bruce Wayne wake in the middle of the night to hear the shots that killed his parents? How many times did he have to face the fact that he could never save them, no matter how hard he tried. Even if he did manage to stop the killer in his dreams, he would have to wake to the cold reality that they were gone and feel the pain of losing them all over again.

Bruce's parents' death would haunt him the rest of his life. So much so, that he would go out into the darkness every night clothed in the colors of mourning ever struggling to stop from happening to other people what happened to him.

Does he ever fail?

Yes.

Every night.

Because he is just a man.

Just like you. Just like me.

No matter how hard he fights, he will never be able to save his parents. The anger he feels toward criminals and corruption are understandable. No matter how many times he locks up the lunatics who plague his city, corruption or incompetence releases them into the streets again. They will hurt innocents and Batman blames himself for every one. They will eventually hurt the ones he loves. On more than one occasion, this harsh reality has come true.

A Death in the Family

In 1988, Bruce's original sidekick Dick Grayson, also known as Robin, grew up and out of his mentor's shadow and became Nightwing who moved to another city called Bludhaven, a sister city of Gotham. One night, in 'Crime Alley,' the place where Bruce's parents were killed, Batman found a young boy trying to steal the tires off the Batmobile. His name was Jason Todd. Bruce took him home and after proving himself worthy of training, he bestowed the mantle of Robin on him and took him on as a partner.

Jason's father was killed by Two-Face and he had never known his real mother. Jason was not like Dick Grayson though. Dick respected Bruce and learned quickly the routine that Bruce laid out for the dynamic duo. Jason was irrational at times, headstrong, angry, and at one point in his life, allowed a criminal to die because he thought it was the right thing to do. Beyond all this, Bruce thought he could make Jason understand that he had to practice restraint and learn to follow his lead.

For some time, Jason wondered who his real mother was and why she left him with his father. In the story "A Death in the Family," Jason got wind that his mother was still alive and wanted to find her no matter what. Bruce agreed to help him in his quest and they set out searching all over the world. They tracked down three different women, all of whom were criminals. After tracking the first and the second down, all that remained was a woman named Sheila Haywood. After finding her, Jason was extremely happy for the first time in his life. That would soon change.

Jason found out that his mother was working with the Joker and was planning to hurt many innocent people. Jason found Bruce in time to warn him. Bruce warned Jason strictly not to take on the Joker alone because he was too dangerous. Batman left. Jason didn't listen.

Thinking he would save his mother, he was actually betrayed by her. After revealing his alter ego to her, she thought he would turn her in to the authorities for embezzling funds from her medical practice. She handed him over to the Joker.

The Joker began beating Jason with such fury and rage that he even brought in a crowbar to kill him. Blow after blow, Jason managed to stay conscious, but just barely. The only thing he could think about was getting his mother out alive. The Joker, in the end, locked both Jason and his mother in the building and destroyed it with dynamite. Both of them were killed.

Batman was too late. He showed up just in time to see the explosion. Sifting through the rubble he found Jason's body, but it was too late. His body was already cold. Batman bore the guilt of losing his partner, his son, to the Joker's malice. Batman would never forgive himself for that.

Batman's guilt drove him on for years in the comics. Batman writers would constantly bring Batman back to Jason's costume over and over again, re-opening the wound he could never heal.

Batman was too late. Robin was dead. Bruce's parents were dead. Bruce was helpless to save them all. He was tormented so much that when the Scarecrow once used his fear toxin on Batman, it drove him to anger instead of fear because of his guilt. Even during the Knightfall saga, when Bane was about to break Batman's spine, he was thrown into Jason's costume's case and was forced to look at his greatest defeat and realize he was yet again too slow and weak to stop the evil from defeating him.

Batman's torment was brought to total confusion when a new villain arrived on the scene. His name was the Red Hood. Originally the costume donned by the Joker before he became the demented clown he is today, the Red Hood seemed to be taking control of the crime in Gotham City.

Not just that, but he also began killing mob bosses and villains Batman faced for years. One night, the Red Hood confronted the Joker who was battling depression in his own life and beat him within inches of death with a crowbar. Afterwards he removed the mask to reveal he was none other than Jason Todd, Batman's lost Robin.

A few issues later, Batman finally confronted the Red Hood on a rooftop of a building. The Red Hood ripped Batman's mask off, then removed his own so Bruce could see that he had returned.

Imagine what that must have felt like to be Bruce. For years, training a sidekick and friend, like a son, and then losing him and blaming yourself because of his death. Then to find out that he is not dead but alive... and a villain. Alfred, upon finding out the truth, asked Bruce if he should remove Jason's costume from the cave but Bruce refused. Bruce's guilt still remains. He can't let go.

Finding Fault and Standing Tall

In *Batman Begins*, Bruce can't let his parents' death off his shoulders. If he hadn't been afraid, they'd still be alive. Or so he tells himself. His anger at himself and the world outweighs his guilt so much that he is willing to take to the streets night after night, seeking the one fight that will end his torment. But he cannot. He will never save his parents. He will never win that battle.

I relate to this on a very personal level. When my grandmother died, I began to look for God. When I started going to church, I thought everything would be alright. I was wrong. I started getting into drugs and alcohol, looking to bury the sadness deep within myself. I couldn't escape.

Night after night, I would dream about my grandmother and the pain she went through before she died. I went to her grave every month and wept for my loneliness and emptiness. You would think after I found God with the church I am at today, I would finally feel peace. But not so.

You see, when I finally found the truth in the Bible, I began realizing how a true Christian was supposed to live. Even though I was changing for the good, I couldn't escape the sadness I felt. I couldn't weigh the decisions I was making with the decisions my grandmother had made in her own life.

I couldn't say for sure that she was a Christian and in the end that she went to heaven. I even had several nightmares where she, while in pain, would blame me for her outcome in life. I was too selfish to learn the truth before it was too late for her.

My grandmother loved me more than anyone I'll ever meet. She took care of me when I was sick with pneumonia even when my parents couldn't be there. She raised me like a son and in my stubbornness I wouldn't seek God until it was too late.

No matter how many people I reach out to, no matter how many souls I share the gospel with, I can never share it with the one person I care about the most. For that I feel guilt and anger. I feel a special sympathy for Bruce Wayne because we share the same sorrow inside. And we both see the fight ahead. No defeat can stop us because we have already fallen victim to it. We press on with perseverance because everything else we care for is at stake.

Standing at my grandmother's grave, I wept bitterly at the conclusions I would have to face in my own life. I had a choice to make. Continue in the lie I was living and suffer the same fate she did or look on to those who still needed my help.

It is the same choice Bruce Wayne faced the night his parents were killed. Looking at my grandmother's name on her tomb, it read Irene E. Gaizat. Covering her first name, I saw the outcome of choosing death over life. I knew my life would never be the same.

I had work to do.

Despite my anger and grief, I had to focus on what was important now and who needed my help the most. Ultimately, that is the same choice I faced when I chose to come into my teen ministry and help the teens there. I would put it all on the line and inspire a new generation of heroes to jumpstart an apathetic church into greatness once more.

There are still times I feel the shadow of grief overcome me. I do not give into these feelings of hopelessness because I know in the end my grandmother would be proud of the decision I made.

And I will continue to make it.

Until the day I die.

At the end of the story of the Red Hood, Jason has decimated Bludhaven and apparently killed Dick Grayson/Nightwing. Holding the Joker hostage, Jason tries to guilt Batman into killing the Joker. Batman refuses to give into Jason's rage. When Jason makes the ultimatum that either he lets Jason kill the Joker or that he must kill Jason, Batman makes his choice.

Throwing one of his batarangs, it ricochets off a pole behind Jason and stabs him in the throat. Jason falls to the ground without a word and is fatally wounded.

Bruce has shown another trait that he clings to no matter what. Even though it was the Joker who killed Jason in the past, Batman could not let himself act out of rage and vengeance. He had to protect the person in need, even if it was from his own adopted son. Bruce knew once he traveled down the path of anger, he would be no different than Jason or Wrath who could not let their anger go.

What in your life do you feel guilty about? Is there sin in your life that you feel can't be forgiven? Why?

Even though I feel motivated by my past, I do not let it control my life. I know from Paul's writings that God reveals himself to everyone so that no one is without excuse for not believing in him (Romans 1:20). My grandmother had her opportunities to learn about and follow God and I know she would want me to make the right choice for myself.

I know there's good that can be done. I know God can use me no matter what I've said, felt, or acted on in the past. If he can use me, he can use you. If you are a Christian, you are already forgiven. If you aren't, forgiveness is not as far off as you think.

Many people feel guilt for the sin they've committed in their lives and have hardened their hearts towards what could so readily be theirs. Abortion, getting or passing STD's, losing someone they love who isn't a Christian for whatever reason, slipping back into an addiction that they thought they'd overcome -- all these things steer us away from what we need the most.

Peace.

Once we are baptized Christians, God no longer remembers our sin and guilt and He accepts us for who we are. We will still mess up, but God's love and plans for us never change in his eyes. Once God declares us innocent, we are forever free from the chains that held us. (John 8:36 – *"If the Son sets you free, you are free indeed."*) We just have to remember that and live like it. Our joy for such a gift is what will motivate us to do what is right and change other people's lives for the better.

And we'll never feel guilty about that.

Chapter 13: Scarecrow – Facing Your Fears

The Master of Fear

Looking at Gotham City, it would not be too hard to imagine being afraid to go outside your doors. Lunatics every night, holding up businesses, breaking out of prison, always attempting mass homicides and tricks to poison the whole city -- who would think of actually living in a city like that? If Batman messes up one time, the city will fall into chaos. It sounds like it would be easy to just lock yourself in your house and never come out because of fear. That's exactly the point according to another of Batman's greatest foes.

Dr. Jonathan Crane was obsessed with fear. Working at a local Gotham University, he watched as countless individuals were put into rooms with the things they were most afraid of and marveled at the power it gave the phobia over the phobic. Soon after Dr. Crane began his experiments, he no longer cared to cure the individual of their fears, but wanted to see what the fear would make the exposed person do when motivated by that fear.

Once the school got wind of his notes and experiments, he was quickly let go and Dr. Crane fled to the streets of Gotham in search of a way to make as much money off of his discoveries as possible. No one seemed to understand his morbid curiosities and motivations. Everywhere he went, no scientist was as interested in learning or sharing in such knowledge of the power of fear.

Becoming more and more desperate, Dr. Crane devised ways to create a fear toxin that would make its victims see and experience their greatest fear. Donning the twisted costume of a walking scarecrow, Crane set out to use fear against his victims and take what he wanted from the city.

Money, jewels, and power were Crane's reward for his ventures as he set out to find more victims. The treasure he longed for the most though, was to watch the effect his fear toxin had on his victims and marvel at the helplessness they experienced as all cowered before their new master. The master of fear. He called himself the Scarecrow.

On more than one occasion, Batman has fallen into the Scarecrow's traps and been subjected to Crane's fear toxin. On some occasions, he has witnessed his parents and other people close to him being killed as he watches in horror and cannot do anything about it.

During the *Knightfall* Saga, an exhausted Batman once again inhaled the fear toxin concocted by the master of fear who was at the time teamed up with the Joker. Instead of being afraid though, Batman saw the image of Jason Todd being killed by the Joker and flew into a blind rage that allowed him to take down the Joker and Scarecrow quickly and easily.

It seems, also, that the Scarecrow often gets to feel the effects of his toxin as he fights the Caped Crusader. Several times in the midst of fights, Crane gets injected, gassed or subjected to his own fear toxins to his defeat. Each time Crane comes back even more obsessed with causing fear and panic among the citizens of Gotham.

There is a difference though, in the fear that Scarecrow creates and the fear people have to live with and overcome every day. Scarecrow enjoys torturing people with their various phobias. True fear, the fear that keeps us out of danger and harm though, can be life-changing and motivating.

Facing the Fear Inside

In *Batman Begins*, Bruce has at one point finally trained his body to the point of perfection. His senses are at their peak. He is nearly one of the League of

Shadows. He has faced his anger but he still has to manage his fear. While it would seem apparent in the film that Bruce has a fear of bats, inside, that is not his true fear. The fear of bats is merely his phobia.

Bruce's true fear was inside himself. He feared his own power and anger, his inward drive to do great or terrible things. His anger could have motivated him to enact his revenge on Joe Chill or kill any criminal who crossed him. His other fear bent on the realization of the challenges that awaited him if he chose to use his power to do something great and change his world.

As Bruce inhaled the fumes of the mysterious blue flower that Ducard made him carry to the top of the mountain in the beginning of the film, it is symbolic of the burden Bruce carried with him. By defeating the power of the blue flower, he could beat the fear he carried with him to the training grounds of Ra's al Ghul. In our Christian walk, we carry many things with us as we make the ultimate decisions to become Christians, including our fears.

What scares you the most? I don't mean what is your phobia? Snakes, heights, spiders, public speaking, and everything else you dread, don't count here. What are you really afraid of? What would be the one thing that could happen to you that would make you turn from God? Can you think of anything? What about if your family was killed in a car wreck? What if you caught a deadly disease that wasn't your fault, like AIDS? Could it be the temptation of getting re-involved with an old flame that you could never say no to? What if you lost everything you owned in a fire and had to live off of scraps for a while until you got back on your feet? What about never being able to accomplish a great dream of yours no matter how hard you try?

They say that the number one fear in America is the fear of public speaking. I can relate to that. To this day, I have led numerous Bible talks, preached about five Sunday messages, street preached five times and led a good number of devotionals.

Some people think I have a knack for that type of thing, but the truth is it scares the tar out of me every time I have to stand in front of a group of people and say more than six sentences. When I know I'm about to speak, I have to say about six different prayers for courage and conviction. I feel like Jesus at the garden of Gesthemane, asking God to take the cup from me.

I really wanted to learn how to preach to large groups but I didn't have a clue where to start. It was then that God put it on the heart of one of our pastors to get a vision for my life that was beyond me. He had started a speaking class in his basement once a week and chose myself, my roommate, and two other guys in the church to learn public speaking.

My first few weeks were horrible. I learned that when I tried to stand on my own, I would fail. But when I included God, praying and letting the Spirit lead me, I would learn and preach better than I ever thought I could. For several months I trained my mind to think like my audience and relate to their needs both emotionally and spiritually.

I had to be able to put aside my boring, emotionless lectures, and tap into the heart of the crowd that was looking for answers and guidance from the scriptures.

I felt like Bruce Wayne being trained by Ducard in *Batman Begins*, facing all the things about myself that separated me from those I wanted to lead. I had to change my weaknesses into strengths. I learned how to read people I had just met so that I could better understand their personalities and their needs. I learned how to look at my own emotions and choose my attitude when my mood would be affecting my judgment.

After several months of training, I was finally ready. I was given my first chance to preach a Sunday message. The title of my message was, "He is not

Ashamed," based off the scripture in Hebrews 11:15-16, where God says he is not ashamed to be the God of men of faith. I had more fun and excitement than I had ever imagined preaching that day. God truly answered one of my prayers by giving Steve a dream for me and my life.

Now, every time I have to face a fear of mine, I can look back on that experience and remember that as long as I remember my place before God, I can overcome anything. That's why the Bible says in Psalm 23:1, *"the Lord is my shepherd,"* and in Matthew 28:20, *"and surely I am with you always until the end of the age."* God is right there next to us, all we have to do is remember that and rely on that.

Facing Your Fears Together

Sometimes we have to face our fears with the help of others. We can provide one another with courage, knowing that those close to us won't abandon us in the midst of trouble or facing our fears. The scriptures say in Ecclesiastes 4:12,

> *"Though one may be overpowered,*
> *two can defend themselves.*
> *A cord of three strands is not quickly broken."*

Many people think that the third chord stands for God. I agree with that wholeheartedly. When I was out street preaching for the first time, I would never have attempted it unless my fellow disciples from my ministry were there. We can also find courage in numbers.

So, have you thought about it yet? What's your worst fear? Bruce Wayne's fear was what he might do with his anger. Would he reduce himself to giving in to his anger and doing something he would regret later? Would he dedicate his life to administering punishment as he saw fit or would he gain control of his anger and keep it in check, even during the hardest of times?

Alone, it would be quite difficult for Bruce. In fact, every time he decided that crossing that line would be the best course of action, someone always steps in to show Bruce that there is a better way. We too, need reminders from our spiritual brothers and sisters that we can overcome our fears and face our challenges and not become what we swore against. Sometimes that person is God speaking to us through His Spirit. We just have to listen and have the courage to stand against our temptations.

Fear can motivate us to do many things we don't really want to do. We compromise so that we don't lose things or push people away that are close to us. We are afraid of being different. We fear public persecution and disapproval. What if our family disowned us because we stood up for our faith? It's happened to Christians before. It will happen again. We have to be ready.

I've never studied the Bible with someone who didn't have to face their fear of something. In fact, I usually define the problem in the midst of studying with people and tell them to be on their guard. Most of the time those exact things happen to them. Sometimes people overcome, but sometimes they walk away from the truth. What about you?

Satan watches us all from afar and plots ways to scare us away from the gospel that will save our souls. He knows exactly when to strike and how. He's been watching us all our lives. Do we see our fear for what it really is? Most of the time, it's pretty obvious. But that doesn't make it any easier to overcome. If it was easy, it wouldn't be a struggle and we wouldn't have to fight back. But as spiritual heroes, that's exactly what we have to do.

Batman, after facing the Scarecrow on numerous occasions, still confronts him regardless of getting gassed with Crane's fear toxin nearly every time. Batman is willing to face his fears and he know it won't turn him away from his mission.

He has courage.

Something Jonathan Crane will never understand.

Now it's your turn. Face your fears. Alone, you may not make it, but if you're a Christian, you have something inside you that can't be defeated. If you aren't you are only a decision away from gaining the Spirit of love, courage, and power that is necessary to fight the spirit of this world, the spirit of evil, darkness and fear.

Those who are with us are more than who are with them (2Kings 6:16) and if God is for us, who can stand against us? (Romans 8:31)

Don't be afraid.

Chapter 14: Harley Quinn – Manipulation and Influence

Good Heart Gone Bad

Dr. Harleen Quinzel was a new psychologist to Arkham. She didn't have a lot of experience but she did have an ear to listen. Besides, interviewing a few big time psychopaths couldn't hurt if she wanted to write a bestselling book on her experiences. Walking down the dark hallways, she gazed into the cells and in the darkness, something gazed back... and smiled.

Upon returning to her office later that night, she discovered a present left for her on her desk. A single rose in a vase, with a note attached, saying "Come down and see me sometime. –J." Deep down inside, Harleen was touched... even if it was by someone like the Joker.

The next day, she went down to confront the Joker. He slyly brushed aside her attempts to be stern about him leaving his cell. As she began to leave, he told her he felt a kinship with her and finally found someone he could share his secrets with. This stopped Harleen dead in her tracks. She thought she would finally get her chance at success in her field... and be there for a patient who she could bond with.

For three months, she studied up on the Joker before she would meet with him so she would be ready for anything. She had immersed herself in the Joker's mind and gimmicks. There was no way she could give in to his tricks. The only question on her mind was why everyone else had given up on him. Was there really no one to understand him like he said?

The Joker began to tell the sad story of his past -- about how his father would beat him in a drunken stupor nearly every day for almost no reason at all. His father had always been that way. Mad and depressed. There was only one time the Joker had seen his father happy -- the time they went to the circus. His father laughed so hard at all the clowns running around pulling down their pants and smacking each other with pies. Seeing his father that way gave him an idea.

One day, when his father was away at work, the Joker took his father's best pants and painted himself like a clown. When his father came home he danced around, dropped his pants and tore a hole in the seam. His father's reaction was instant. He broke the Joker's nose and beat him unconscious. His father didn't get the joke, the Joker said... just like Batman.

Harley was moved to tears but tried to hide it from the Joker. She believed the Joker was just a victim of circumstance and was just lashing out for love and affection. A lost child who wanted the world to laugh at his antics. Why did everyone have to leave him alone? Couldn't they see he just needed someone to care about him? The Batman, so self-righteous, only wanted to torment the Joker and make his life a nightmare. Why couldn't anyone else see this?

As unprofessional as it was, after so many months of talking and sharing stories and listening to the Joker, she fell in love with him. As she grew up and focused so much of her life on being professional, her inner longing for someone to make her laugh and care about finally manifested itself in the form of Arkham's most famous inmate.

Once, the Joker escaped from Arkham to lash out on his uncaring world, alone and scared. Apprehended and bullied by the evil Batman, the Joker was returned to his cell again, given up on by the world to be locked away where everyone could forget him. Everyone but Harleen. As she witnessed the guards locking her love away, she decided she was going to act.

Stealing a costume from a local costume store, she drove secretly into Arkham, sneaking by all the guards. When the coast was clear, she broke the Joker out of his cell. When the Joker realized it was his Harleen, she told him to call her Harley Quinn, his new sidekick, apprentice, and girlfriend. The two have been at large ever since but this is not the end of their story.

The Whispers of Satan

Harley's actions are not totally unbelievable or uncommon to tell you the truth. In fact, I've seen a whole lot of Harley Quinns in my life as a disciple. Her fault lies not in her heart or lack of actions, but in her ignorance and ease of manipulation.

The Joker does not love Harley. He does not care about her well-being. He doesn't even want to share his life with her. But he knows he can string her along with lie after lie, influencing her to do whatever he wants. All he has to do is push her empathy button until she bends to his will.

Let's take a look at Harleen's story. First of all, she's inexperienced. That means she won't see the Joker coming. He spends his life trying to outwit Batman; a naïve psychologist will be a piece of cake. Second, she's lonely. She's young, professional, and ambitious.

If she had been older she may have had time to have some fun in her life but because she's young, she's sacrificed to be where she is. Her 'go-get-em' attitude means she'll be willing to listen, even if it is only what she really wants to hear. It may take time... but she'll be broken eventually.

Joker's sob stories tugged at her heart strings until she could no longer resist the charms of the clown prince of crime. If she only knew the joke was on her.

Before I get to the end of this story, let's take a deeper look into the problem with people like Harley, because it is so easy for people to become like her. Let's talk about influence and manipulation.

It's not hard to be manipulated in our culture today. Simply turn on the television, crank up the radio, go to work, hang out with your friends, pick up a comic book... need I go on? We are constantly being influenced. Whether we want to or not, it's happening. We take in so much of our surroundings, it's no wonder we can be so *easily manipulated.*

Don't believe me? The Bible says bad company corrupts good character. (1Corinthians 15:33) So let's take a look at ourselves. When we hang around worldly people at work or in school, even if it is just our friends and they are swearing all the time, isn't it easy to have a slip of the tongue and curse ourselves?

When we're around scantily clad women or men, especially in the summer time or spring break or even when we see sexually explicit content on television, movies or the internet, don't we find ourselves struggling with purity issues more frequently?

Be honest.

And why shouldn't we want it? The world constantly tells us we need these things. We have to have someone hanging off our arm to be important. We don't have the rest of our lives to find the one person meant for us. After 35, don't your chances of finding someone go from zero to nada? Your youth pastor obviously doesn't understand. After all, they're married, right? They don't know how hard it is to be a teen in this decade. Don't be alone... at all costs... don't be alone.

I stand here in the light, beckoning you: Don't listen to that voice.

If the world didn't find people to believe its lies, it would die. Its methods would be proven false and people would not fall into the traps that solidify their sin, trapping them in bad situations for the rest of their lives. Am I being too harsh? Let's look deeper.

Manipulated By Desire

A brother I was close to, began having an interest in a fellow student at the university we attended. She wasn't a disciple, but because he didn't deal with his feelings, he began to grow attached emotionally. They began studying every day, sometimes more than once a day, for hours at a time together.

The rest of our ministry, myself included, didn't see the brother so much for a period of time, but we just thought he was busy, because the semester was ending soon. We all had our workloads to deal with and our classes to pass. Eventually he started bringing the girl to our spiritual events. It was then that he began confessing his feelings for her to the brothers and me.

It didn't take long before word got out to the rest of the ministry. We tried to help him with his feelings but whenever he tried to pull himself away he became angry and violent, even at points breaking things in his apartment because they couldn't be together. The leaders of our church even became alarmed at what he was feeling and doing.

The girl studied the Bible and eventually became a Christian. We thought their struggles would be lightened but it only got worse. The ministry planned an event at the girl's house one weekend. We had a great time, but after we all had left, the brother returned. The two became impure together and fell into immorality.

They both vanished for days.

I remember waking one morning to find my roommate leaving for school. I didn't know it but the brother was in the apartment at the time and sat me down to break the news. It had been such a struggle for the brother that I felt he didn't even have to tell me what they had done. I already knew.

They ran off and got married.

They got scared because of their fear of what the leaders of the church would say. So they eloped, leaving their brothers, sisters, friends, and family out of the picture and taking matters into their own hands. I was upset and devastated at the same time. Why had they done this? Why couldn't they be open and honest about their lives? Why didn't they fight their urges?

Simple. They were influenced. Satan singled out the brother for months, planning his time to strike just when he was the weakest. The Bible says that Satan walks around like a lion, looking for the one he can devour.(1Peter 5:8) His lure was simple. The pretty girl, a chance to hide his sin and the chance to make his wish a reality.

Well, at least they are still together, right?

Aren't they still happy?

Three weeks later they filed for divorce. The new apartment they lived in became her home as he left out on his own. She would never talk to any disciple who wanted to help her. Neither one returned to the church for fear of persecution. How wrong they were. In the end, Satan got what he wanted.

Two more down.

What Would it Take?

What influences you? Money? Music? Movies? The internet? Television? Love? A pretty face? The media? Attention? God? Death? Anger? Lust? A chance to escape from your problems? What is it?

You have to face this just as much as your worst fear. It is the hinge on your door of salvation. Satan will try to exploit this weakness.

Expect it.

I study the Bible with people all the time and when I see what hump they have to overcome to become a true disciple of Christ, I warn them in advance that Satan will use that against them. I am almost always right, and unfortunately, most of the people who say to my face that they won't fall for Satan's schemes, play right into his hands and give in to those very temptations I warned them about.

I'm not even immune to such attacks from Satan. When I first became a Christian, my biggest fear was that my ex-girlfriend would come back asking me to run away with her.

I always fell for her before I became a Christian, no matter how bad I felt about our relationship. Sure enough, 3 months after I became a disciple, she showed up at my work telling me how she was leaving her husband because she missed me. By myself, I was not strong enough to face this conversation, so I interjected someone who could: God.

I told her all about my conversion and what it took to get me to that point. Part of me really wanted her to come to the same conclusion I had about my faith, but after our conversation, I didn't hear from her for another six months.

So I faced one of my greatest fears and guess what? When I brought God into the conversation, I won against Satan's schemes.

Ask yourself: "What would it take to make you fall away from God?"

Seriously. Think about it. Write it down. Look at it and imagine what it would take. If you can see it then you can face it. Face it then you can overcome it. Overcome it and you can help others with the same weakness. Help others... and you're a hero.

We have a great example of what the Bible says happens to an influenced society. Look at Romans 1-3. The Romans were filled with all kinds of ungodliness and it was beginning to influence the way the church conducted itself.

The same is true for the Corinthian church, only they put value on spiritual gifts. If you didn't have the right gift you weren't that important. It's scary but true. Only when Paul confronted them on their ungodliness would they attempt to change.

Let's not wait for the godly to challenge us on the influence in our lives before we do something about it. We all need a reality check from time to time or else we'll end up like Harley Quinn, lost in her naïve fantasy world that the Joker fashioned for her. The Joker is a lot like the false prophets talked about in 1Timothy 4:3, where Paul tells the church:

> "The time will come when men will not put up with sound doctrine. Instead, to suit their own desires, they will gather around them a great number of teachers to say what their itching ears want to hear."

The Joker is only telling Harley what her ears want to hear. By doing so, he gains another loyal servant to his cause. The world is no different. Satan will try to tell you whatever you feel you need to hear to make you his forever. Don't let yourself be blinded by your desires in this world.

At the end of the Batman episode, Batman reveals the Joker's true intentions to Harley but she won't listen. Even when the Joker shows up, he smacks her around, yells at her, and throws her out of a third floor window onto a garbage heap on the ground. She tells herself it was her fault and that she didn't get the joke like the Joker's father.

Even when she is confronted by the Joker's true nature, she still kids herself into thinking the Joker still loves her because he sends her a flower in her cell when she is captured. Harley won't let herself see the truth because she wants the lie that badly.

Fight the lie. The world only has sadness and pain to offer. Maybe not now, but definitely in the end. The world will lure you in, tear you apart and leave you stranded alone, and without God.

We are lucky we serve a gracious, forgiving God who will accept us back, even when we don't deserve it. (2Corinthians 1:3) Harley could find redemption if she really wanted it, she just has to stop listening to the empty promises told to her. Don't be like Harley. Let your influences be from the example set before us by our master and Lord, the Christ.

This is your wake up call.

Chapter 15: Catwoman – Honor Among Thieves

"I told you recently there was something different about you. Now I know why. You care for her. Maybe... even love her. Your mysterious opponent knows this and will use that against you.

Is she worth it?" asked Talia.

"... yes..." whispered Batman.

-Batman and Talia in *"Hush"* [k]

The Bat and the Cat

Batman and Catwoman's relationship has been a complicated one since the two first met. Ever since the first appearance of Batman in 1939, the Catwoman has been around causing mischief in Gotham City.

Selina Kyle's life has been a troubled one. With almost no recollection of her young life, her struggles have taken her to the streets, the home of gang boss, Carmine Falcone, prison, the Hall of Justice, and both in and out of hope. As retold in the graphic novel, *Batman: Year One*, Selina Kyle first appears as a tough prostitute who savagely fights to protect her sister.

Selina has given up on having a better life. Inspired by the Batman's influence on society, she dons a cat-like costume, deciding never to go back to selling her body but unlike Batman, she turns to stealing what she wants as a cat burglar.

After years of battles with Batman and the pursuit of wealth, Selina eventually lands on her feet, no pun intended. Seeing the error of her ways, she even for some time, teams up with Batman to help him fight crime. While many are suspicious of her motives, the one person who never seems to mind her being around is Batman. Even during a short spell, when Batman would not let any other crime fighter run the streets of Gotham, he still let Catwoman lend a hand.

Why would Batman let this one time villain turned hero run the streets to fight crime and not even his own partner, Robin? What makes her so special to Batman? What does she have that the others don't?

Batman's heart.

It's true. Batman is head over heels in love with Catwoman. For years, Bruce has known Selina's secret but it wasn't until recently that he has decided to share his own with her. During the Hush saga, Bruce brought Catwoman to the Gotham Zoo and removed his mask for her to see who he was.

Bruce did it because he needed to share the deepest part of his life with her for her to accept him. He knew that even as they went on dates as Selina and Bruce that she was always thinking about Batman and that she really wanted to be with him. She cared for Batman more than she ever let on with him. She even tried to stop him from ruining his life by killing the Joker.

Bruce considers himself and Selina to be two sides of the same coin. He sees that their fates as intertwined for a reason. He wants to help her but the pursuit is bumpy because they both have pushed others away for so long that they can't commit to each other for fear of distrust and betrayal.

The Bible describes love in 1Corinthians 13:1-7,13:

"If I speak in the tongues of men and of angels, but have not love, I am only a resounding gong or a clanging cymbal. If I have the gift of prophecy and can fathom all mysteries and all knowledge, and if I have a faith that can move mountains, but have not love, I am nothing. If I give all I possess to the poor and surrender my body to the flames, but have not love, I gain nothing.

Love is patient, love is kind. It does not envy, it does not boast, it is not proud. It is not rude, it is not self-seeking, it is not easily angered, it keeps no record of wrongs. Love does not delight in evil but rejoices with the truth. It always protects, always trusts, always hopes, always perseveres.

And now these three remain: faith, hope and love. But the greatest of these is love."

While Bruce may think he loves Selina, his pursuit for her is ultimately doomed. His love cannot become like that which the Bible describes.

Chasing a Cat's Tail

I too, know what it is like to pursue a doomed relationship. In my senior year of high school, I dated a girl who I thought I was head over heels for. We spent a lot of time together although much of it was not healthy in the biblical way. The one time I really wanted to impress her was at my senior prom.

It was the first major dance I had been to in the four years I was in high school. I had my silver and black tux and my date had her silver one piece dress and we spent a ton of money for that one special night. We had a great time with all of my friends, and we even went on a carriage ride downtown afterwards. The only thing that was left was the trip to the nearby amusement park the next morning.

I was pretty restless that night, waiting to go with the girl I thought I loved and as soon as five o'clock in the morning hit, I called her to wake her up. To my surprise she answered on the first ring. That's when the big disappointment hit. My best friend was on her other line.

The two of them had been seeing each other for some time. I was crushed. How could the two people I cared about the most do this to me? All trust I had with the two of them was gone. I couldn't even look anyone in the eye because I felt about an inch tall. Even my grandmother tried to comfort me, as she always did, but I was devastated.

Some time passed and I realized some very important things. One was that I was not in love. I enjoyed the sinful pleasures my relationship brought but it was in no way as fulfilling as the true love the Bible spoke of. To tell you the truth, it took a long time before I could begin to trust again.

Through much of my spiritual walk, I butted heads with my brothers in Christ many times because I was so fearful that the men closest to me would try to betray me. I almost drove myself insane trying to keep everyone around me in check so they couldn't do anything bad to me or hurt me again.

I needed the trust that comes only from the spirit of peace.

A peace that passes all understanding.

Trusting in God, Not Ourselves

In John 13, Jesus puts a heavy burden on the shoulders of his Apostles. They have just received news that one of them will betray Jesus to his death. While arguing over who it was and who was Jesus' greatest follower, Jesus washes his disciple's feet, to their shame. Next Jesus tells Peter that they are all going to desert him despite their arguments otherwise. Disheartened, Jesus told them in John 14:1,

> "Do not let your hearts be troubled. Trust in God; trust also in me."

Trust did not come easily for Jesus' twelve. Doubt filled the hearts of Jesus' disciples nearly every time something challenging arose. Jesus' example was to show them that God would not give up on them. His last words to them on Matthew 28:20 were that surely he would be with them always, to the very end of the age. He knew they struggled with trust.

When I met Crystal, the girl I would marry, I had a very tough choice to make in my life. I had to trust God that she was the one for me and that she would choose me over several other brothers who were trying to pursue her heart. I had to forget my struggles with my best friend and my ex-girlfriend.

I had to forgive my brothers in Christ who in my mind, always seemed to try and woo the girls I thought I cared about. I needed to trust God. So whenever I started to feel anxious, I would imagine Jesus looking me square in the eyes and say:

"Trust in God. Trust also in me."

Whenever I struggled with my anger...

"Trust in God. Trust also in me."

When I felt the world weighing on my heart...

"Trust in God. Trust also in me."

When I needed God to intervene in impossible situations...

"Trust in God. Trust also in me."

When I had to confront sin going on in my ministry and I felt insecure...

"Trust in God. Trust also in me."

By trusting in Jesus and in God's plan, my faith grew. I learned to let my emotions stop controlling me and trust God. I could confront the sin in my life with hope that I could change. The day I finally put my trust in God, as far as my possible relationship with Crystal went, was the day that we started dating steadily.

Victory at last.

Jesus came through for me.

All he asked for was my faith and that it would be so.

Now I am happily married to my true love, my wife Crystal. We have a small house, a dog, a teen ministry, and a God bigger than us both, watching out for us.

Where is your faith?

Can you hear Jesus asking you to trust in his will?

Trust is the first step toward faith, and faith as small as a mustard seed can throw mountains into oceans.

Batman can never have Selina's heart completely. Situations always arise that bring up distrust and feelings of betrayal from both sides. Batman will keep fighting for her feelings and against his own. Selina's wounds go deeper than her trust to let Bruce or Batman make her drop her guard. Until Selina can get beyond her past, she is doomed to be alone.

Selina does not have the peace that passes understanding. She will always doubt the love of her life and insecurely push him away. In the same way, Batman is doomed to keep everyone at arm's length so that he won't feel the guilt that comes with defeat and loss.

Even Bruce's love cannot overcome because it is not the love that can conquer all. Both Batman and Catwoman's trust lies solely in themselves, not through faith that can make their relationship work. That is why they are doomed to fail.

Trusting and having faith in God can give us the confidence and courage to know that we are victorious as long as we draw strength from knowing God has the ability to overcome everything we can't.

Listen to the voice of the one who calls...

"Trust in God. Trust also in me."

Chapter 16: Riddler – Riddled with Pride

"Well, Sully, riddle me this... What do you get if you never take a risk? ... absolutely nothin'."

-Riddler – *Batman: Hush Returns* [I]

The Enigma of Edward Nygma

Edward Nygma was different from all his classmates. He was a gifted problem-solver. He could solve any puzzle, riddle, and joke before the punch line was even given. For years he studied cryptography, history, and things others would call useless facts, just to gain an upper hand in knowledge over his classmates.

This caused Edward to become very unpopular with the in-crowd. He got picked on all the time growing up and despite his superior intelligence, making the bullies feel stupid was not a wise thing to do.

At home, Edward would find no rest either. His father was an abusive drunk who thought Edward's obsession with games was a waste of time. Why couldn't he take an interest in sports like all the kids his father knew growing up?

Deep down inside Edward wanted to please his father. He didn't like being kicked around by bullies at school. But Edward knew he would never fit in with the popular kids at school. His intelligence made him smarter than even the geeky kids. Once Edward reached the end of his high school career, his outlook on life was about to change.

Edward started using his vast intellect to outwit his classmates and make people feel inferior. His father's influence and intimidation made Edward's venting all the more potent. Soon his only pleasure was outwitting his own teachers and making others look like fools intellectually. His self-confidence boomed as he continued to learn more and more about the world.

Getting fed up with being poor, he ran away from home and began looking for ways to scrounge up money. It didn't take him long to figure out how to use his riddles and tricks to scam money from people. After a few short months, he began to devise ways to make bigger heists against stores and richer folks to gain even more money. But the money wasn't enough. He wanted more.

He had read in the newspapers about the new dark figure Batman and how he had outwitted criminals of all kinds. Edward deduced that Batman must be very smart to have outwitted some of Gotham's finest minds and always stay two steps ahead of their detectives.

Edward decided to put his vast knowledge on the line against Gotham's greatest detective. Creating a costume of his own, Edward wore a green suit covered in question marks and a purple mask. Dubbing himself the Riddler, Edward would leave notes with riddles in them for Batman to find and see if Batman could figure them out in time to stop his heists.

Crime after crime and riddle after riddle, the Riddler matched wits with Batman, each time making it harder and harder for Batman to solve. In the end of each scenario though, the Riddler's game always proved to be inferior to Batman's skills. It was then that a new riddle would obsess the Riddler... whose great mind hides under the cape and cowl?

The Riddler kept trying to find out who Batman really was. It would take many years and a losing battle with cancer before he would find out who Batman was. Undergoing a trip to a Lazarus Pit by the villain Hush, the Riddler was reborn with a new sense of clarity. Using all the information he had available to him, he actually deduced Batman's identity as Bruce Wayne and concocted a huge scenario to challenge Batman to his core and face his greatest defeat... the death of the second Robin, Jason Todd.

After the series had ended, Batman confronted the Riddler and Edward revealed how he had discovered Bruce's identity. Batman's response guaranteed that the Riddler would never reveal this information. For Riddler had defiled one of Ra's al Ghul's Lazarus Pits, and to do so meant one thing... certain death. If Edward revealed his identity to anyone or used it to his advantage, Batman would let Ra's know who used his Pit.

The Riddler was defeated again.

Pride vs. Confidence

The Riddler's overconfidence goes way past his lust for money. In the beginning of his career, he stole to survive. His puzzles were just a gag to fool the police. Once Batman stepped into the picture, it became something much worse. It became a pride issue.

Nygma had never met anyone who was his equal mentally. Even his greatest peers lived in Edward's shadow. It was his only ability that could make him stand above everyone else. It was the foundation on all he stood for -- his ability to confuse, confound and trick anyone he came into contact with. When Batman began to solve his riddles and outsmart Nygma, it became more than just a game.

Riddler's pride is not only his greatest drive but his greatest weakness as well. Batman outsmarts Nygma because he too, has trained himself to study how others think. Riddler's puzzles and attempts to discover Batman's identity were simply games Bruce had to figure out to deter the Riddler's plots. Batman succeeded for one simple reason.

Confidence.

Batman has the confidence it takes to figure out the Riddler's plots. He knows it is just a matter of time and patience before he outsmarts Edward. He never gives the Riddler the opportunity to gloat over his riddles which only seems to drive the Riddler to be even more obsessed to try again. It almost seems this cycle will never end as the Riddler keeps trying to outwit Batman and fails.

In our walks as Christians, we often face the battle between these two character traits. One is a sin and the other is not. If you were to ask any number of disciples what they struggle with the most, a good number would probably say pride.

Honestly, we should fear the sin of pride. It makes us do selfish, foolish things that we otherwise would not do. We hide behind our pride when we are embarrassed, humiliated, or joked at. We can deny advice from those who are wiser than ourselves or not want to confess our sins because we feel it will make us look bad. We use it as a shield when others cross a line that make us feel vulnerable. We fight to hold onto our dignity even if it makes us look even more foolish.

Have you ever had an argument with someone who wouldn't admit they were wrong? I once had a couple of friends who got into an argument over a silly card game. After about ten minutes of hearing the argument, I went upstairs to watch a movie with another friend. When it was over we went back downstairs and saw that they were still arguing over the same card move at the time I had left. Their pride was so overwhelming; they both looked pretty foolish after an hour and a half worth of arguing over one card move.

Godly Pride vs. Worldly Pride

Is there such a thing as good pride? We hear people say "I'm proud of you." Is this a selfish, bad pride or a healthy expression of love? Can you be confident without being prideful? There is a difference, but we have to look beyond the surface of our emotions.

Worldly pride leaves us bitter and hurt. We lash out at others because we don't like to face the fact that we may be wrong. We may try to prove our point so much that in the face of being proved wrong, we explode into a ball of fury and storm away to our own disgrace.

Godly pride gives us the chance to be confident and brave. Godly pride allows us to celebrate our victories and still stay humble enough to know where our victory comes from. Knowing God is proud of us can make us very confident.

The Bible says in James 4:6, that God opposes the proud but gives grace to the humble. It also says in Hebrews 4:16 that we should approach the throne of grace with confidence. But where do we draw the line so we don't fall into the bad kind of pride?

Looking at a scripture in 2 Corinthians 7:2-4, 8-13:

> *"Make room for us in your hearts. We have wronged no one, we have corrupted no one, we have exploited no one. I do not say this to condemn you; I have said before that you have such a place in our hearts that we would live or die with you. I have great confidence in you; I take great pride in you. I am greatly encouraged; in all our troubles my joy knows no bounds.*
>
> *Even if I caused you sorrow by my letter, I do not regret it. Though I did regret it—I see that my letter hurt you, but only for a little while— yet now I am happy, not because you were made sorry, but because your sorrow led you to repentance. For you became sorrowful as God intended and so were not harmed in any way by us. Godly sorrow brings repentance that leads to salvation and leaves no regret, but worldly sorrow brings death.*
>
> *See what this godly sorrow has produced in you: what earnestness, what eagerness to clear yourselves, what indignation, what alarm, what longing, what concern, what readiness to see justice done. At every point you have proved*

yourselves to be innocent in this matter. So even though I wrote to you, it was not on account of the one who did the wrong or of the injured party, but rather that before God you could see for yourselves how devoted to us you are. By all this we are encouraged."

In the first set of scriptures, Paul tells them he takes great pride in them and that he has great confidence in them. Then he tells them about what our sorrow should produce in us as Christians. Facing our sin with confidence, we can take our sin seriously and when we have overcome, feel no regret. It is when we face our sin with the bad kind of pride will only take us to the darker side of ourselves that eventually leads to death.

Have you ever been so disgusted by your sin that all you can think about is how to make things right again? Have you ever lost sleep because you just had an argument with your best friend before you went to bed? There's a reason why we can't sleep, can't eat, can't concentrate when we know we have done something wrong. We lack humility and God is staring at us in the face, asking us why we won't make things right.

That is why when we humble out and confess our sins, do we feel the times of refreshing that God has wanted us to have all along. (Acts 3:19) Then we can feel the confidence of knowing that God's way works and that as long as we follow his path, he won't give up on us.

Did you know that God is a wall of fire around us? (Deuteronomy 4:24) For someone to even touch us, they have to put their hand through God. The Bible says, *"if God is for us, who can stand against us?"* (Romans 8:31) He chose us and predestined our lives to be his children, the brethren of Christ and heroes of the world. (Ephesians 1:11) These scriptures alone should make us borderline cocky toward the forces of evil in our lives.

Even David, in 1 Samuel 19, when facing the towering Goliath, exerted a confidence in God that surpassed understanding. In the end God used David, a boy, to humiliate the Philistine and bring down the armies that blasphemed the name of the Lord. God even raised up David to humiliate the king of Israel, Saul, for his lack of faith.

And therein lies the key of confidence.

Faith.

Faith in God.

And God's faith in us.

Confidence is the fresh air we breathe as we renew our strength and take our stand against Satan and his followers. Pride only gives us reasons to run away and hide. With pride we think we're on top, but our confidence in God and his plan will set us above the rest.

Riddle Me This...

Think about what it must be like to be around someone with the confidence of Batman. He knows he will be victorious over the Riddler's schemes and plots because in the end, Edward Nygma's pride will overtake him. The Riddler makes his greatest mistakes in his attempt to wield his pride as a weapon against his inferior foes. Batman just makes the Riddler's weapon too big for even him to wield and eventually the Riddler's pride topples right over him. And we've all heard the saying, "pride comes before the fall."

Now imagine what it's like to be around the Riddler and his pride. It wouldn't be very encouraging to be around someone who always thinks he's right and tries to put himself one step above everyone around him. Yet we all know people like this. They are very lonely people who only find comfort in their own achievements. They will not be outdone by anyone and they make sure people know it.

The only way to escape becoming the Riddler and being more like Batman is to consider others better than ourselves and to have a humble servant's heart. When we serve others and make them feel important, we can gain many friends in our fight to free people from their pride.

Jesus even demonstrates this when he washes his disciple's feet in John chapter 13. Imagine Jesus, God in the flesh, on his hands and knees washing your feet. He knows his place among creation but he wanted to give us an example that we can imitate to wake us so we can see where we really stand before other people.

If we can tackle our pride and use humility and respect to see who we really are before God, we will gain the confidence in our lives to be heroes like David, who knew that the real battle was God's, not man's. Then we can be more like Batman and less like the Riddler.

If God is for us, who can stand against us?

Not the Riddler.

Not Satan.

We've won.

We can take confidence in that.

Chapter 17: Ra's al Ghul – Leadership at its worst

Back to the Garden of Eden

Of all the Batman villains, I've underrated Ra's al Ghul the most. Passionate and driven, Ra's has lasted for centuries, shaping human events and history trying to accomplish one goal. Eradicate sin from the earth.

Using his assassins, called the League of Shadows, Ra's has trained some of the best warriors known to man. Quick, brutal, exact, determined, loyal, and deadly are qualities that can describe any one of Ra's subjects. They perform without question, even to the death if it served Ra's goals.

Centuries ago, Ra's had a normal life. He lived with his wife and daughters in the mountains of Asia. Ra's had helped the prince of his city from dying by discovering a life-rejuvenating pond that healed his prince's wounds. Incurring madness along with his new life, the prince killed Ra's wife and sentenced him to death for her murder in his place. Ra's escaped execution. Banding together his relatives, Ra's returned and killed the prince for his treachery.

Exacting revenge on those who killed his wife, Ra's came to one simple conclusion. Evil must be faced head on, without mercy, without compassion. Law did not work. Men were too easily corrupted to handle the eradication of evil. He would have to do it himself.

When he confronted his wife's killers, Ra's discovered that the death of sin was the only way to find peace. But could he train his men to carry on his work after his death? Ra's knew his work would never be done in his lifetime. So fate showed him a way to keep him alive.

Returning deep within the Earth, to the springs of life, a fountain of youth so to speak, the aging Ra's nearly collapsed in its wake. His men thought he was dead for a moment but then the fallen leader came springing back, youth restored and lashing with rage. Once he could be subdued and gain his right mind back, Ra's realized his potential to go on and change the entire world.

Dubbing the pool the Lazarus Pit, he devised a way to conquer entire cities and lands and restore the world to its original state -- back to the days of the Garden of Eden. When sin was wiped out entirely, then mankind could have a chance at redemption.

For centuries, Ra's and his men burned prominent cities like Rome and London. He took credit for the fires of Chicago and disasters of epic proportions. In our present day, he also spread a deadly virus amongst Gotham and its people.

In Ra's empire there was but one rule. For anyone else to use the Lazarus pits except for him would mean certain death. For once one Lazarus pit was used, its rejuvenating properties would be spent. He had tracked down hundreds of Lazarus pits throughout the ages and only a few remain to this day.

During a time when Batman and Robin found their way into Ra's territories, the young Dick Grayson was mortally wounded and the Assassin's leader, out of respect for Batman's great mind and deeds, allowed him to place Dick Grayson into the pit for rejuvenation, draining the pit of its energies.

Realizing Batman's goals of ridding evil from his city, Ra's became very interested in making Bruce one of his subjects and tried to teach him the ways of the League of Shadows. Bruce, upon discovering Ra's schemes of destruction, escaped the clutches of his foe and returned to Gotham. Ever since then however, Ra's has put his focus of destruction on Batman's great city.

For years, Bruce and Ra's have battled each other, putting the fate of the entire city on the line through every encounter. Each time Ra's has lost and in doing so, used many of his Lazarus pits to stay in the game. Each time he returns, Bruce knows he is going to be put to the test and stretched to his limits. If he fails one time, all of Gotham will fall forever.

The Deception of the Great Trainer

Ra's al Ghul has a very twisted view on how to handle sin. He does very great things both the right way and the wrong way. His methods are extreme but his thinking is not. Let me explain...

Many great leaders in the past have tried to wipe out what they consider sin in their generation. The ones who go about it in such harsh and extreme ways are the ones who are most vividly remembered. Such instances you may recall are Pharaoh slaughtering the Hebrew children because they grew too numerous and he feared an uprising.

Herod wiped out thousands of children trying to find the Christ. Hitler tried to kill millions of Jews in concentration camps to bring about an "ethnic cleansing." Even in our own day, Saddam Houssein used biological weapons in his own country to try and wipe out his enemies.

Mass graves are, in history, not as uncommon as you would think. Putting in the word genocide into a search engine can bring about all kinds of historical accounts of sad, terrible things that men have done. When one race unites to destroy another because of simple disputable matters, all that can follow is horror.

Ra's al Ghul has been hardened by the anger in his heart. He may try to refute the icy chill in his heart but his actions speak far greater than his words. He has lost something great to him. He will not lose it again, no matter what the cost. Trying to bring the world back to the days of the Garden of Eden, Ra's has forgotten that this too, has been tried before.

In the days of Noah in Genesis 6, God sends a great flood wiping out humanity, sparing but four couples to replenish the Earth with people. Did those eight people bring about the change in the world God wanted for us all along?

No.

In fact, because of the sin of Ham, Noah's son, his offspring were cursed forever. Even Noah himself got drunk on too much wine and lewdly went about his business.

Sin was not gone.

Man's nature had not changed.

God himself wiped out Sodom and Gomorrah, raining fire upon the towns, saving only Lot and his family. Surely there was no more sin after that! Sadly, this is not the case. Lot's daughters got their father drunk and committed incest with him, disgracing themselves as God's people.

And when God went with the Israelites to conquer the promised-land, the Israelites wiped out the towns and everything in them to set themselves aside as holy amongst the nations of the world. When they didn't fully obey God and they saved things for themselves, they would lose battles and suffer plagues for their short-sightedness.

The land the Israelites conquered was not nearly as large as it was supposed to be because they didn't follow God's instructions. This is not to say they weren't a great nation but sin cheapened the whole deal God had planned for them. They were supposed to wipe out sin but instead they incorporated it into their lives.

Just looking at Noah's example, we see that wiping out the human race or even a portion of man, does not change the nature and desires that dwell inside all of us.

If Ra's did succeed, how long do you think it would take for mankind to be as corrupt and sin-filled as it is right now? Not very long. So what can we learn from Ra's flawed thinking?

First, we will never be done with fighting sin. Sin is not a nation that can be subdued and wiped out. We can drop spiritual nukes on ourselves all day long, but as soon as we take a breather, sin will come back to haunt us. How long can you go without sinning? A day? A week? A minute? A few seconds? So if we can't destroy the sin in our own lives, what can we do about the sin of the world?

Remember Jesus took it to the Cross.

God tells Cain in Genesis 4:7 that sin is crouching at his door and it waits to have him but he must master it in order to overcome. We fight because we know we must master our sin. But we can only go two ways.

Master it, or be devoured by it.

Take great care in knowing that you can master your sin if you can first understand both your nature and your motivation. Our nature tells us we can't escape our sin. In one degree this is true. We focus on one sin only to be attacked from a different angle we didn't even notice. But that doesn't mean we stop fighting.

God gives us the healing and refreshing during our times of repentance to strengthen us to keep fighting. (Acts 3:19) Our motivation comes from knowing that we have God's grace as breathing room to comfort us in our times of sin so that we will not become burdened and will keep fighting.

Leading Vs. Lording

Ra's keeps fighting because whether or not he is truly insane, he believes he is right in his methodology. Clashing with both Batman and Superman, Ra's always manages to escape death and capture, leaving him to plot his diabolical plans over and over again. His intense learning and skills make him one of Batman's deadliest villains ever. But despite all that he does, he cannot do anything without his loyal subjects.

Ra's way of leading is very extreme. Crossing his path or plan once means a quick death. His way is the only right way. All else is foolishness and delaying the inevitable. He knows how to deal with sin. Cutting off your right hand, if it causes you to sin like Jesus mentioned, would be tame compared to Ra's' surgical strike to the body.

To Ra's credit, he does hate sin. So much so that he is zealous to overcome the world. His men's loyalty to him only fuels his mission and they believe in his ways as much as he does. Looking in, one might say he is a great leader. In a worldly way they are correct. In a godly way though, this couldn't be further from the truth.

Ra's lords it over all mankind to fall to his plan. Ra's doesn't take into consideration the innocent. In his mind, the innocent only exist to become perpetrators of crime, violence, and sin in the future. This makes his task that much easier not having to look at his own faults and heart.

In this world, there are two types of people: leaders and followers. There are many followers and fewer leaders. It's easy to fall into the crowd mentality and not think for ourselves. We trust our leaders because they are appointed above us in many instances like our jobs and schools. In church it is not that much different except we nominate and appoint our leaders from within because we believe they will guide us on the path God has chosen for us. When this happens, we rejoice. When this is not the case, we have a problem.

Ra's example of sinful leadership is not as uncommon as we wish it could be. Selfish, bitter, and prideful leaders in our fellowship are inevitable. Satan fights against them as much as any of us and there are times when some will fall. How we think on our own will determine the fate of our fellowships.

If a leader refuses to acknowledge sin in their lives or the damage they may have caused, it can be very discouraging, especially when they are removed from the fellowship by the congregation. What can we do in times like this?

We have to remember to work out our own salvation with fear and trembling. (Philippians 2:12) This is not a call to walk away from our church when times get tough. This is a call though, to remember that we have a duty to not just follow our leaders but help them when they are down, just like they should help us when we are down.

We are all human and share the same nature. Satan will not attack the strong with weak advances but with equal force. For every action, there is an equal and opposite reaction. This goes the same for Satan and his schemes.

Once in a campus ministry I attended, the leader of our group kept using our discipling times to call out sin in the ministry. I felt betrayed nearly every week as he exposed my sin to the group, trying to convict the rest of the ministry.

Our times of sharing and confessing were supposed to be private. He would never use my name in the preaching but the examples were just too close to home for me. I struggled wanting to be open with my leader for a long time. Often times, just telling him everything was okay so that I didn't have to hear about it the following Friday.

I eventually got open with another brother in my ministry to how I was feeling. He challenged me to go back to my leader and confront him on my feelings. I didn't think I had the right. He was above me in the "leadership food chain." How could I call him out on what I think is wrong? I was a lot like the followers of Ra's al Ghul. It didn't matter what I thought because I had a hierarchy of importance in my mind. He was higher than me; therefore, my input didn't count.

How wrong I was. After a few days of prayer and meditating, I confronted my leader with my feelings. He apologized deeply and was sorry that he had hurt me and our relationship. In the next meeting we had, he even confessed it to the group and we continue to have a good relationship to this day.

Ra's al Ghul will not change if someone doesn't stand up to him and show him that his sin is just as devastating as the next man's. On many occasions, Batman has tried to show him the good side of humanity but Ra's will not move from his mission.

Jesus appointed twelve people to rule over his church when he was gone. All these men had different styles and in many cases, different views as to who and what Jesus came to do. In time they would get it right but Jesus had some kinks in their character to work out. Looking at his apostles, let's look at one example that Jesus would use to define the term: Leader.

> *"It was just before the Passover Feast. Jesus knew that the time had come for him to leave this world and go to the Father. Having loved his own who were in the world, he now showed them the full extent of his love.*
>
> *The evening meal was being served, and the devil had already prompted Judas Iscariot, son of Simon, to betray Jesus. Jesus knew that the Father had put all things under his power, and that he had come from God and was returning to God; so he got up from the meal, took off his outer clothing, and wrapped a towel around his waist. After that, he poured water into a basin and began to wash his disciples' feet, drying them with the towel that was wrapped around him.*
>
> *He came to Simon Peter, who said to him, "Lord, are you going to wash my feet?"*
>
> *Jesus replied, "You do not realize now what I am doing, but later you will understand."*

*"No," said Peter, "you shall never wash my feet."
Jesus answered, "Unless I wash you, you have no
part with me."*

*"Then, Lord," Simon Peter replied, "not just my
feet but my hands and my head as well!"*

*Jesus answered, "A person who has had a bath
needs only to wash his feet; his whole body is
clean. And you are clean, though not every one of
you." For he knew who was going to betray him,
and that was why he said not every one was
clean.*

*When he had finished washing their feet, he put
on his clothes and returned to his place. "Do you
understand what I have done for you?" he asked
them. "You call me 'Teacher' and 'Lord,' and
rightly so, for that is what I am. Now that I, your
Lord and Teacher, have washed your feet, you
also should wash one another's feet. I have set
you an example that you should do as I have
done for you. I tell you the truth, no servant is
greater than his master, nor is a messenger
greater than the one who sent him. Now that you
know these things, you will be blessed if you do
them."*

-John 13:1-17

Did you know that in the New Testament, the
term leader is interchangeable with the word servant?
Here we have twelve students of the ultimate teacher
and in his time of distress over who was going to betray
him, these men began arguing over who was greatest.
They just didn't get the message.

So God himself got down on his knees and
showed them that in his kingdom, to be the greatest
meant to be the most humble, not the one with the
highest rank. To lead meant to serve. To serve meant to
set the example. It would be some time before his men
would get it but in the end, they would all give their
lives for the chance to serve the church.

This example is one that Ra's will never understand. If men would not serve him, he would have no choice but to change. But since he is left unchallenged and served by his men, his power trip continues.

Ra's task may appear over when he runs out of Lazarus pits, but history has proven that there were leaders who came before and after him that share his same philosophy. At times, we may feel that our church, our ministry, or our brothers and sisters are going in the wrong direction. Sometimes sin can seem bigger than ourselves, but if we have a heart that cares about our leaders and our ministries, we can come to help even those we hold in high regard.

Let's not give up on those God appoints over us as leaders. When they mess up, we have to be as willing if not more, to forgive them as we would those sitting next to us on Sunday morning. The call for all of us is to serve, repent, and to help others. If that means a leader has to take a step down for a while, then so be it. Remembering we are all on the same playing field as God sees us, we don't have to be intimidated by the status forced on us by society and sometimes our own minds.

We all live to be examples in this life. Good or bad. In this way, we all live to lead those who we would inspire to be like us.

Let's do it like Jesus would... not like Ra's al Ghul.

Chapter 18: Poison Ivy – Worshiping the Created

"Are you starting to resist? Foolish. No man can resist me. Now come closer so I can remind you what will make me happy..."

-Poison Ivy – *Batman: Hush* [m]

Poisoned by Nature

Dr. Pamela Isley was a specialist in botanical biochemistry. Among her peers, she stood alone as the greatest mind in her field. Growing up in a wealthy family, she was able to attend the greatest schools in Gotham. For years she fought against the "glass ceiling," that held back so many of her female classmates as her male colleagues looked on.

One such individual was a man named Jason Woodrue. He admired Pamela from afar and watched her research grow beyond anything anyone ever expected. He also saw the monetary significance this would have on anyone who had the technology. Stealing her notes and files, he would try to sell the information on his own. One thing stood in the way -- Pamela Isley.

Impersonating their lead professor at the University, he tricked Pamela into injecting herself with a deadly neurotoxin that should have killed her in moments. As Jason left her to die on the floor, Pamela's body began to convulse and change. Her vital signs ceased twice during her poisoning but when her body stopped struggling against the toxin, she did not die. In fact, her body was changed forever into a hybrid plant-woman. She became known as Poison Ivy.

Experimenting on herself, she found out that her body chemistry and makeup was changed drastically into what seemed more plant than human. Her skin could be poisonous to the touch by any other person, her lips, even secreting a neurotoxin of its own that could either critically poison her subject or control their actions.

Her skin itself could change to a green or pale white color depending on her mood. Her experimentation on plants and herself gave her the unique ability to control plants and plant-animal hybrids by both thought and word. No longer seeing herself as part of a human society, she became a misanthropic individual, shunning herself from society and its barbaric laws and societies.

Instead, she became so obsessed with plants that she made herself believe that a world ruled by plants, not man, would be the best reality of all. Becoming an eco-terrorist, Poison Ivy began taking on Gotham's big businesses that were bent on destroying what was left of its natural wildlife and habitats.

Thwarted by Batman on several occasions, Poison Ivy will not give up on her goal of conquering the world and ridding it once and for all of humans and their anti-nature ways. She is obsessed and she will not give up until she breathes her last botanical breath.

Seeing the Forest for the Trees

Pamela Isley, or Poison Ivy, has a twisted view on the world and what its goals are. She has given up on her humanity to embrace something that she holds close to her heart -- the environment. While this in and of itself is not bad, her obsession with it is.

Poison Ivy struggles with the sin of idolatry -- in more ways than one. Her motives are all based on the lifting up of plants and oppressing humans. This might seem to make her anti-social or anti-technology but in a more simple way, plants are all she sees. She has immersed herself so deeply in her world that she cannot see the forest for the trees anymore, so to speak. All she sees are ways to strike back at an uncaring cruel world that seems to not care about her floral paradise.

Her obsession with plants has proven to be her downfall. She knows everything about plants. Names, places of origin, botanical make-ups, hybrids, species, and every other little aspect that many people would never care to learn, she knew. And ultimately, by creating her own hybrids that she can control, she is in fact playing god in her own little world.

Strangely enough, Pamela's obsession also includes children and her maternal instincts. Due to her body's reconfiguration, she can no longer have children and on some occasions, she has gone out of her way to protect orphans and children who are lost, looking for their parents. She often instead refers to her plants as her children.

Pamela Isley is not so different than so many people we meet, especially here in America. Idolatry is very rampant in a technologically rich world where people have the means to obtain almost anything they desire or want. People in the industry often obsess with, "If we don't have it, we'll make it, then make it better and everyone will **have** to buy it."

Eventually our wants become our needs and we fall into a vicious cycle to not just have something, but to have the newest, best one on the market.

Technology isn't the only way people become idolatrous. Sports, video games, collectibles of all sorts, cars, gardening, cooking, and even through other people do we turn from God and his ways to worship something else. It's not hard to find out what those things are in our lives -- just think of what you feel like you can't do without.

Write those things down on a piece of paper and really think about whether or not you could live without those things. Don't even read on until you've answered this in your mind.

So what did you come up with? Your computer, your car in the garage, your favorite article of clothing, your pet, or your television? Did you even think about your mom, dad, or siblings? What about your Bible? Did God even enter your thoughts? This might be a warning sign that you might be focused on the wrong things in this life.

Now don't get me wrong, I'm not saying there is a right or wrong answer here but I am trying to pry open your heart and see what makes you tick. Many things you may have thought about may have sentimental value.

I have my own things as well, like my skateboard signed by my favorite skateboarder or my box containing all my comics that I've used to put together this book or even my laptop on which I'm writing these pages now. My favorite Batman figures surround my desk my home computer sits on.

They are important to me sentimentally but if I have to choose one thing to take with me, it's not going to be any of those things. I know I can get those things back. My writings are backed up on the internet so I can get them back. My Batman figures aren't going to keep me warm at night. My comic collection is replaceable. My dog and car are both replaceable. (Sorry Chi-Chi!) My wife though, is not. I made a vow to honor, protect, and cherish her beyond all things... all things except God.

We idolize anything by putting it before God, even at times, ourselves. Some people spend their whole lives as though the universe revolves around them and they are sure to point that out to everyone they meet. Have you ever heard the stories of celebrities having extravagant lifestyles that include insanely demanding things be done for them? One famous rapper even paid someone to separate his candy into colors and separate bowls after every show he performed! Some people spend tens of thousands of dollars to have the perfect body (Whether it is plastic surgery, piercings, or tattoos).

When they are all finished, what do they look like? What do you see? Is it a perfect human or a shadow of what God designed them to be, like Poison Ivy versus Pamela?

Is there anything you put before God? I myself am not exempt from scrutiny in the least. I have had my battles with idolatry both before I was a Christian, and after I became one. My idolatry usually took the form of a girl that I would like. After I became a Christian, I would try to be spiritual just to get their attention and I would be insanely jealous of the girls I liked before I became a Christian.

At times I would play video games days on end never once thinking of picking up a Bible or saying a prayer. The scriptures say all good things come from God (James 1:17), but wisdom also tells us that too much of any good thing can be bad for us.

The ultimate weapon against idolatry is surrender. If we can surrender our thoughts, attitudes, and motives to being content with what God has given us, we can conquer that empty feeling we have that gives us that feeling of craving for more. True surrender is only a clear choice away from discontentment and the defeat of our idolatry.

Let's see what else the scriptures have in store for us.

Cast Down the Idols

Throughout much of the Old Testament, Israel's predominant sin was that of idolatry and worshiping of idols from other nations. Punishment for their deeds included two exiles and even the flood of Genesis 6 and wiping out of cities like Sodom and Gomorrah. Another example of punishment against the nations was the Hebrew invasion of the Promised Land, showing the surrounding nations that the gods they served were simple creations of man from wood and stone, had no real power.

We look back on the Israelites and read of their foolish natures that gravitated to simple idols and away from the God of the universe, and we laugh. Well, the joke's on us too, then. We look around and see people obsessed with everything else around us except for God. How are we any different than the Israelites of the Old Testament?

Want to know if you fit into this category? Here's a challenge. What's your favorite sports team? Can you name all the players? Good. Now name all the apostles. Can you do it? Can you name all the stats for all those players, but struggle with memorizing verses in the Bible that can help you shape your life into what God wants you to be?

I don't want to pick on the sports-a-holics out there. What about those of you who idolize someone special in your life. What is their favorite color? What do they like and dislike? What are the six things God hates and seven things that are detestable before him? If you want to know, God tells you in Proverbs 6:16-19. Will you devote yourself to someone else and forget God?

What about you who read comics? Do you know everything about the characters of the pages you read, but neglect the character of God? This book, in fact was not to show how Christianity applies to Batman but how Batman applies to Christianity. There is a difference. Do you spend so much time in your imaginary world that you let the world around you fall into decay?

Saul, the first king of Israel, fell because of idolatry. See for yourself in 1 Samuel 15:22-23:

> *But Samuel replied:*
> *"Does the LORD delight in burnt offerings and sacrifices as much as in obeying the voice of the LORD ? To obey is better than sacrifice, and to heed is better than the fat of rams.*
>
> *For rebellion is like the sin of divination, and arrogance like the evil of idolatry.Because you have rejected the word of the LORD, he has rejected you as king."*

Saul's arrogance was like idolatry towards God and for that, God removed Saul and replaced him with a man after his own heart, David.

Idolatry is one of the sins in Galatians 5:20 that will block us from entering the kingdom of God. Paul even goes on to say that greed is a form of idolatry. (Colossians 3:5) The love of money is the root of all kinds of evil. People will do all kinds of things for money. Some can never have enough. Money provides a false sense of security. We need to remember that we rely on our faith to get us by. Otherwise, we scramble and tear at each other because we have removed God from our sights and think we can accomplish keeping ourselves safe on our own.

There's no shortage of causes that can consume our focus and attention away from our Creator. It's amazing though, the level of hypocrisy that comes across so many people who are trying to do 'the right thing' with their causes.

Talk to animal rights activists and ask them their view on abortion. Most are for abortion, the killing of human children, but for saving animals from 'atrocities' committed by men. These people can't even tell you that a mosquito is less important than your own family. It's a sad state of affairs, truly.

Peter reminds the church of their old ways in 1 Peter 4:1-5, when he says:

"Therefore, since Christ suffered in his body, arm yourselves also with the same attitude, because he who has suffered in his body is done with sin. As a result, he does not live the rest of his earthly life for evil human desires, but rather for the will of God. For you have spent enough time in the past doing what pagans choose to do—living in debauchery, lust, drunkenness, orgies, carousing and detestable idolatry. They think it strange that you do not plunge with them into the same flood of dissipation, and they heap abuse on you. But

they will have to give account to him who is ready to judge the living and the dead."

The world will not understand why you don't indulge in such things as they do. I've had friends who have pleaded with me to go back to my old life. They don't understand when I tell them that before I came to know God, I really didn't have a life or not one that I could ever see myself returning to. Can I forget the truth? Can I really turn my back on God and return to the things that I was obsessed with before without so much as looking back? Even if I could, what good would it do me or anyone around me? All that would be left would be my selfish desires.

Poison Ivy herself could use her plants to make humanity better. She could help create cures for illnesses that appear to be incurable. She could use her blood as an example of how to make humanity immune to sickness and disease. She could use her plants to remind people of how beautiful nature could be, but instead she hoards everything for herself and lashes out at anyone who even tramples grass in the wrong way. She has given up on making the human world a better place and in doing so, she has given up on her humanity as well.

Until she can break her fixation on her plants as her only means of happiness, she is forever doomed to fight for the things she loves more than anything. All we can do is try to not be like her and so many others in this world and fix our hearts on things above (Colossians 3:1-2). We can come to the conviction of 1:Corinthians 6:12, which simply says:

"Everything is permissible for me"—but I will not be mastered by anything."

Let's remember that there is one God that we serve.

He is a jealous God who will fight for us.

Let's fight for Him.

Chapter 19: Bane – Sins of the Father

"Born to life and a life sentence, behind the walls of Pena Duro. This is not the story of how Bane was born. It is the story of his creation."

Batman: Vengeance of Bane [n]

The Bane of Gotham

In the comic, *Batman: Vengeance of Bane*, a new villain was born --one that would challenge Batman on more than just one level. Taking a deeper look into Bane's motives and history, we see a deeper root behind his methods.

On the island of Santa Prisca, civil war was a way of life. Revolting factions would attempt to take over the country and one by one they were defeated by the ruling government. Bane's father was one such faction leader. After a three day battle in the capital of the city, their fight was over. Bane's father was killed in combat; however, this was not the end of his family's suffering.

Bane wasn't even born yet, his mother still waiting to give birth. Bane had one chance. If he was born a girl he would have been released from prison. But fate had other ideas. Bane was born a male and the government's laws stated that Bane must serve his father's life sentence.

Taken to Pena Duro, the hardest prison in the country, Bane grew up in confinement. It was all he knew. His mother eventually passed away from despair after eight years. From that moment on, Bane was on his own. After being nearly assaulted by another inmate, Bane fell over a railing and landed on his head, knocking himself unconscious. In a vision, Bane saw himself as he would be growing up. The urge to fight back as his father had done was planted deep inside of him. When Bane awoke from his unconsciousness, his childhood was over.

Approaching the man who tried to assault him earlier, Bane committed his first murder at the age of eight. As punishment, Bane was sentenced to solitary confinement for ten years. Most other prisoners in his situation succumbed to death or madness. For Bane, there would be no surrender. Confinement was all he knew. He learned to be patient, to stalk the animals that entered his cell by land or water and exercised his body and imagination constantly. When he was let out, the warden was disappointed to find that the boy, now a man, had not surrendered to death.

Being released into the general population, Bane became a model prisoner. He was allowed to work in the library and a fellow inmate, a man from Gotham City, nicknamed Birdie, taught Bane to read and write. Birdie filled Bane with stories of the Batman and how he ruled Gotham's night and used terror to control his city. Bane vowed to come to Gotham and defeat the menacing Bat that had begun to plague his dreams. Defeating the terrifying Batman became his obsession and he began plotting the day he would finally confront the harbinger of fear in Gotham.

Bane needed to practice his new skills of instilling fear and fighting. Killing nearly thirty men in the prison over a short period of time, the warden ordered Bane be taken in and brought down to be tested using a new super-human strength-enhancing drug that had killed every other inmate tested. The substance was dubbed Venom. Unlike all the other prisoners, the Venom did not kill Bane as his body built a tolerance to the side effects. Bane now had a weapon that made him stronger than anything he had ever known. In Bane's mind, he was perfect... but he was not free.

Bane's friend, Zombie, altered Bane's drug to give him the appearance of death. When the warden thought Bane was another failed experiment, he had his body thrown into the ocean. When the effects of the drug wore off, Bane was outside the compound. But Bane did not leave the island. Instead, he returned to rescue his friends and to grab the warden. Stealing a helicopter, Bane and his fellow escapees fled to Gotham, but not before dropping the warden to the sharks as he had done to Bane's mother's body.

At last Bane would get his chance to defeat the great savior of Gotham and make his mark in the world. He would rule Gotham with his dedication and iron grip on all crime in the city.

It would not take Bane long to devise a plan to ultimately break the Batman physically and mentally. Over the next few months, Bane would destroy Arkham Asylum and free every criminal Batman ever caught. For weeks, Batman had exhaustively recaptured all the escaped inmates and handed them over to the new prison, called Blackgate. When he had finally finished, Batman was exhausted. But upon returning home he found that Bane was there waiting for him.

Bane had deciphered who Batman really was and toyed with the Dark Knight as he used his venom to overpower the weak Batman and break his spine. With Batman broken, Bane would try and claim rule over Gotham.

It would seem his father's influence in his life had finally found victory in Gotham.

Like Father, Like Son

Bane and Batman really aren't so different in their core drive. Bane's father's goal was to overthrow the government that enslaved his nation. Bane's goal was to overthrow the fear that gripped the criminals of Gotham. Bane finally succeeded where his father failed.

Batman's father also had a great influence on Bruce's life. Thomas Wayne was a surgeon and fought every day to save people's lives. In *Batman Begins*, Alfred tells Bruce that his father nearly bankrupted Wayne Enterprises trying to combat poverty. Bruce's battle, as the Batman on the streets of Gotham, is his way to combat the evil in his city in response to his father's example.

In the Bible, we have another Father/Son relationship we can reflect on to give us guidance. Jesus was the Son of the one and only God. He lived his life by his father's example and tried to show mankind how things were supposed to be done -- kind of like Batman's example to Gotham to fight back against the evil that haunted them. Both Batman and Jesus were experts in their situations.

As our heavenly Father, God tries to inspire us and encourage us to overcome the sin in our lives by giving us his Word, the Bible. We look to it for encouragement and guidance. The Bible doesn't hide the fact that the world is an ugly place and often it feels like an uphill battle. It does though, remind us we are on the winning side and keeps us on the narrow road. Jesus had all kinds of things to say about his relationship with his father. Here is one of my favorites:

> *"Jesus said to them, "If God were your Father, you would love me, for I came from God and now am here. I have not come on my own; but he sent me. Why is my language not clear to you? Because you are unable to hear what I say. You belong to your father, the devil, and you want to carry out your father's desire.*
>
> *He was a murderer from the beginning, not holding to the truth, for there is no truth in him. When he lies, he speaks his native language, for he is a liar and the father of lies. Yet because I tell the truth, you do not believe me! Can any of you prove me guilty of sin?*
>
> *If I am telling the truth, why don't you believe me? He who belongs to God hears what God says. The reason you do not hear is that you do not belong to God."*

(John 8:42-47)

Jesus tells the difference in the children of God and the children of Satan, who are the children of the world and its desires. It is the same difference between Batman and Bane. They both live for their father's purposes. One simply does it to help, the other to hurt.

Jesus doesn't hide his feelings about his Father, his goals, or his mission. We have to have this same feeling about our heavenly Father, but sometimes we get tripped up because of our view of our own fathers here on earth.

In my own life, my father was only around until I was nine. Then he revealed to our family that he had been cheating on my mother and that he wanted a divorce. My father had struggled with sexually oriented sin for as long as I can remember. He had stashes of pornography in his closet and had paintings of naked women on his bedroom walls.

I saw my father infrequently as I grew up but I struggled with my purity greatly when I stayed with him. After I became a disciple, I moved in with my father to help him pay his bills as I went to college. One night I came home to find my computer riddled with a virus because he had used it to download pornography.

It took about a month to get rid of all the viruses on my computer and I was very mad at my father for his carelessness and disrespect for my wishes as a disciple. Confronting my father on his sin was not something I was used to or comfortable doing.

I had not struggled with internet pornography... ever until after that time. I'm not sure what it was that got my attention but my struggles with purity ventured to the computer after that. After confessing it to a brother close to me, I knew what I had to do. I had put off confronting my father on the sin we both now seemed to share. I always seemed to think of the age-old excuse for my actions as, "Like father, like son." But I didn't want to follow in my father's footsteps. Not in this area, but I kept failing. I seemed to share my father's fate, just like Bane.

I wrote my father a note about three pages long, detailing all the things he had done to hurt our relationship by downloading all the viruses to my computer and how I struggled with my purity because of his tolerance of sexual sin in our household, not just at the time but growing up.

That night, my father and I had the best talk we had ever had in our relationship. He promised me that he would not use my computer again except to check email and encouraged me to put a password protection on my computer to safeguard myself.

I wish I could say that my influence thus far has helped my father overcome his sin, but to this day it has not. To overcome my sin, I had to start living for my other father, the one who gave me forgiveness for my sins. The one who fought Satan himself and died for me so that I could live to help others overcome the same sins I would have to face myself.

While my father hasn't become a disciple, he has started to change his actions and has even started attending our Bible talk group every other week. If that wasn't enough for God to prove himself, my mother and step-father also attend the same group meetings. So in the group I lead, I now include my father, mother, and step-father, all of whom get along great. Now THAT's God working.

When I started to grasp the idea of using my struggles to help others in the same circumstances, I could finally begin to face my purity issues and break myself out of the habit of blaming my father for my failures. Blame-shifting was the selfish way to deal with my sin and not make myself look bad. I had to realize my failures were mine and mine alone. God would help me out of my struggles but I had to want to change. Thanks to God, I did.

Our Sin Passed On

Did you know that in some denominations, they teach that it is proper to baptize babies and newborns to relieve them of their inherent sin from Adam. The scripture they use to back this up with is in Romans 5:12-13. It reads:

> "Therefore, just as sin entered the world through one man, and death through sin, and in this way death came to all men, because all sinned- for before the law was given, sin was in the world."

This doesn't sound right to me as a Christian. We all mess up enough in our lives to warrant our own punishment, that to think we are born sinners is ridiculous. If this is true, why does Jesus say to enter heaven, we must be like children. (Matthew 18:3) Jesus also scolds his own disciples for trying to turn away children from coming and learning from him. (Matthew 19:13)

If you still aren't convinced, perhaps the chapter of Ezekiel 18 will convince you. It reads:

> "The word of the LORD came to me: "What do you people mean by quoting this proverb about the land of Israel:
> 'The fathers eat sour grapes, and the children's teeth are set on edge'?

> "As surely as I live, declares the Sovereign LORD, you will no longer quote this proverb in Israel. 4 For every living soul belongs to me, the father as well as the son—both alike belong to me. The soul who sins is the one who will die.

> "Suppose there is a righteous man who does what is just and right. He does not eat at the mountain shrines or look to the idols of the house of Israel. He does not defile his neighbor's wife or lie with a woman during her period.

> He does not oppress anyone, but returns what he took in pledge for a loan. He does not commit

robbery but gives his food to the hungry and provides clothing for the naked. He does not lend at usury or take excessive interest. He withholds his hand from doing wrong and judges fairly between man and man. He follows my decrees and faithfully keeps my laws. That man is righteous; he will surely live, declares the Sovereign LORD.

"Suppose he has a violent son, who sheds blood or does any of these other things (though the father has done none of them): "He eats at the mountain shrines. He defiles his neighbor's wife. He oppresses the poor and needy. He commits robbery. He does not return what he took in pledge. He looks to the idols. He does detestable things. He lends at usury and takes excessive interest. Will such a man live? He will not! Because he has done all these detestable things, he will surely be put to death and his blood will be on his own head.

"But suppose this son has a son who sees all the sins his father commits, and though he sees them, he does not do such things: "He does not eat at the mountain shrines or look to the idols of the house of Israel. He does not defile his neighbor's wife. He does not oppress anyone or require a pledge for a loan. He does not commit robbery but gives his food to the hungry and provides clothing for the naked.

He withholds his hand from sin and takes no usury or excessive interest. He keeps my laws and follows my decrees. He will not die for his father's sin; he will surely live. 18 But his father will die for his own sin, because he practiced extortion, robbed his brother and did what was wrong among his people.

"Yet you ask, 'Why does the son not share the guilt of his father?' Since the son has done what is

just and right and has been careful to keep all my decrees, he will surely live. The soul who sins is the one who will die. The son will not share the guilt of the father, nor will the father share the guilt of the son. The righteousness of the righteous man will be credited to him, and the wickedness of the wicked will be charged against him.

"But if a wicked man turns away from all the sins he has committed and keeps all my decrees and does what is just and right, he will surely live; he will not die. None of the offenses he has committed will be remembered against him. Because of the righteous things he has done, he will live. Do I take any pleasure in the death of the wicked? declares the Sovereign LORD. Rather, am I not pleased when they turn from their ways and live?

"But if a righteous man turns from his righteousness and commits sin and does the same detestable things the wicked man does, will he live? None of the righteous things he has done will be remembered. Because of the unfaithfulness he is guilty of and because of the sins he has committed, he will die.

"Yet you say, 'The way of the Lord is not just.' Hear, O house of Israel: Is my way unjust? Is it not your ways that are unjust? If a righteous man turns from his righteousness and commits sin, he will die for it; because of the sin he has committed he will die. But if a wicked man turns away from the wickedness he has committed and does what is just and right, he will save his life. Because he considers all the offenses he has committed and turns away from them, he will surely live; he will not die. Yet the house of Israel says, 'The way of the Lord is not just.' Are my ways unjust, O house of Israel? Is it not your ways that are unjust?

"Therefore, O house of Israel, I will judge you, each one according to his ways, declares the Sovereign LORD. Repent! <u>Turn away from all your offenses</u>; then sin will not be your downfall. Rid yourselves of all the offenses you have committed, and get a new heart and a new spirit. Why will you die, O house of Israel? For I take no pleasure in the death of anyone, declares the Sovereign LORD. Repent and live!"

So God himself has released us from the burdens of our father's sin. He knows that punishing someone for the sins of their father is unjust and unfair. Bane's captors believed the exact opposite and it turned Bane into the murderous anarchist he is today. Whenever we turn our lives against God's teachings, we stand to become the very things we profess to be against.

For this reason, Bane's acceptance of his father's lifestyle and sin will forever keep him on his path of destruction. Batman's acceptance of his father's choices to make the world a better place has won him the title hero over and over again. In the same way, we must dedicate ourselves to our heavenly Father's goals for our lives and imitate his Son who gave us the perfect example of how to be godly in our lives and have a great, positive influence on our world.

If we have to choose a father's example to follow, let's choose the one who has the best in mind for us and show the world whose family we truly belong to.

Chapter 20: The Joker – Face Your Arch Nemesis

"You must see the reality of the situation. It's all a joke! Everything anybody ever valued or struggled for... it's all a monstrous demented gag! So why can't you see the funny side? Why aren't you laughing?"

- *The Joker - "The Killing Joke"* [o]

Batman's Arch Nemesis

Light cannot exist without darkness. Good cannot exist without evil. Ultimately, according to Dick Grayson, Batman cannot exist without the Joker. They are two sides of the same spectrum.

Batman is order.

The Joker is chaos.

Most people don't know or understand the Joker's origin. I am speaking of the comic Joker, not the film version portrayed in the 1989 film. The Joker's origin is not far from Bruce Wayne's tragic beginnings. One simply chose one path at the end of the crossroad. The other went the opposite direction.

Prior to the story, "The Killing Joke," the Joker's history was virtually unknown to the world. The only thing not revealed in this story about the Joker is his name. In Legends of the Dark Knight #50, a cousin of Joker's starts to call him a name starting with "Ja..." but finishes by calling him "Cousin Joker."

Despite his "happy" demeanor, the Joker's origin is actually quite sad. Some time ago, he had a wife who was pregnant and due to give birth to a baby boy. To make ends meet, he worked in a chemical plant as an engineer. His job started getting to him so he had to make a decision. During a stressful point in his life he quit his mundane job and tried his luck as a stand-up comic. The problem was that he wasn't very funny, and a boring comic doesn't get very many jobs.

Once his new career started struggling, so did the bills. His marriage was still strong though. His wife loved him through the thick and thin. All he needed was the money to get out of their crummy neighborhood and into a better one so they could raise their child with dignity. Unfortunately for him, he chose the wrong way to do it.

He caught wind of a couple of thieves who worked for a crime syndicate running through Gotham. They were very successful and very rich. Going for the big score, he agreed to help the thieves break into the old chemical plant he used to work for and to steal enough money so he could leave his life of poverty. He lied to his wife, telling her he was out working, when he was really out planning his big crime.

The night of the robbery, his destiny was about to be fulfilled. Putting the last few details into the heist, police officers approached him at a bar. They weren't there to question him about the robbery.

They came to tell him his wife was dead.

As his wife was attempting to fix a bottle heater, there was a short in the electricity. Both she and their unborn son were killed instantly. Now he had no reason to go on.

He attempted to get out of the heist, but the crooks strong-armed him into going ahead with the plan, saying if he didn't they would kill him. He agreed and as they left, he buried himself in his grief. Everything he truly valued in his life was gone.

When they got to the chemical plant, he was given his identity for the night -- a bright red helmet that covered his whole head. He would become the Red Hood, a popular gang leader of the crime syndicate. Every night the crooks went out, they made their newest member the unofficial "leader" by making them wear the

Red Hood getup. This was actually the way the thieves got themselves out of trouble, by blaming it on the poor sap in the costume, should they be caught.

During their entrance, it wasn't long before the armed security spotted them. They attempted to flee but the two thieves were gunned down before they could escape. They were trying to hit the Red Hood as well but a dark black figure told them to hold their fire. It was Batman, a new costumed vigilante who preyed on the criminal element in Gotham. As Batman approached the Red Hood, he had but one chance - to jump into a vat of chemicals and swim to the streams outside. Jumping over the railing, he dove into the green chemicals and like a baptism of fire, was born again.

Standing in the rain that night, as he discarded the helmet from the burning flesh around his head, he stared into a puddle and embraced his new life -- not as a rich crime boss, not as a stand-up comic, or a chemical engineer, but as a creature of chaos and insanity.

The Sad Cold Truth of the Joker

For the Joker, there was no one to turn to. Life had dealt him a hand and only the jokers were wild. With no ties left to his old life, he sought a new one -- one that would show the world that the only answer to the meaningless humdrum of life was to go crazy. Anything else was to truly be insane. Batman opened the door and would be the demon that haunted him ever since. It would be Batman that the Joker would truly mock in his existence.

The Joker has always stood against everything Batman has tried to preserve. To the Joker, the law was a set of rules for ordinary men, and if Batman can walk around those lines, so can he. If Batman could inspire others to stay in those boundaries, then he could cause them to scatter. It is not enough for the Joker to kill his enemies and cause fear and panic in the streets of

Gotham. He has to show Batman that he is wrong. He has to show Batman that in the end, given the circumstances that make them who they are, mankind will naturally go toward chaos.

Batman and the Joker aren't really that different you see. Both lost their families to cruel and unusual events, very suddenly. The difference is in the decision they made afterwards. Bruce had someone to help guide him along the way, and although Alfred is imperfect, he did provide the love and support Bruce needed to make the right decisions in his life.

The Joker had no one. Bruce chose to dedicate his life to making sure as few people as possible had to go through what he did. The Joker would dedicate his life to making as many people like him as possible, in death and in life, scarring his victims with a chilling smile through his toxic laughing gas.

For years, Batman and the Joker collided in battle, one always getting the upper hand on the other. It is unknown how many people have fallen to the Joker's twisted schemes. Each victim is another face to add to Bruce's nightmares. Bruce knows in the end, it will come down to one killing the other.

In "The Killing Joke," Batman goes into Arkham to confront the Joker and make amends with him, offering any help he needs, even a friendly ear to help him recover from whatever he has been through.

The Batman says:

> *"Hello. I came to talk. I've been thinking lately. About you and me. About what is going to happen to us in the end. We're going to kill each other, aren't we? Perhaps you'll kill me. Perhaps I'll kill you. Perhaps sooner. Perhaps later. I just wanted to know that I'd made a genuine attempt to talk things over and avert that outcome. Just once."*
> [p]

At that point, Batman realizes that he has been talking to someone impersonating the Joker and that his nemesis is free on the streets. That same night the Joker, in an attempt to kidnap Commissioner Gordon, shoots his daughter Barbara who is also Batgirl in the stomach, paralyzing her from the waist down. He then takes Gordon to an abandoned carnival and tortures him, trying to make him go insane and prove that anyone who loses everything, just like he did, would naturally go insane.

When Batman finally tracks the Joker down, he replays the conversation he was supposed to have in his head as he is fighting the Joker. At the same time the Joker starts talking to Batman, wondering why his nemesis isn't as crazy as he is.

Batman comes crashing through a mirror behind the Joker with the response:

"Because I've heard it before... and it wasn't funny the first time." [q]

Batman knows he wants to help the Joker but the situation dictates that they continue their struggle. When the Joker finally runs out of ammunition, he gives up and awaits the beating he is expecting. Batman then took the opportunity to reach him despite his horrendous acts that night. He tells the Joker he wants to help him.

The Joker thinks for a minute but declines Batman's offer. He chooses to take the suicidal course they are both on and ride it until it's over.

Defeating the Joker

Who does the Joker represent? Satan? Can you relate or determine who in your life is like him? One would think from the title of this chapter, I was going to talk about Satan. Yes and no. While Satan definitely tries to throw our lives into chaos and break our spirits, I think the Joker is more like many people we know.

Paul writes in Philippians 3:18-19:

"For, as I have often told you before and now say again even with tears, many live as enemies of the cross of Christ. Their destiny is destruction, their god is their stomach, and their glory is in their shame. Their mind is on earthly things."

There are enemies of the cross of Christ. We have to understand this if we are going to face our enemy. While it is God's will for everyone to be saved, we face a dark, deep-rooted evil in men's hearts that we must fight against.

It is not difficult for the world to gain allies. Apathy, greed, debauchery, lust and hatred all too easily convert those naïve to the darkness to its heinous ways. How many children does Hollywood taint with their twisted views of the way they think things should be? How many people are influenced by the garbage spilling forth from radios and televisions that tells them that their lives are meaningless and pointless without fame and wealth through whatever means?

How many children die as a result of abortion because sex is sold through any medium and is taught to be "the norm," because if you aren't doing it, you're a loser?

How many of our friends and loved ones turn to alcohol or drugs to get them through a hard day instead of a heart to heart with a brother or sister in Christ? It's easier to ignore the problem than to face it. It's easier to throw the bill away and pretend you never got it than to pay it. Even if they have lost everything like the Joker, which direction do they turn?

Good is hard.

Evil is easy.

How easily do our atheistic companions gain allies? I've seen it in my own life. A godless person fighting a struggling believer into questioning what they really believe and causing that person to think everything they've been taught is a lie. For someone who is not ready, it never seems like it's that difficult to be challenged and confused.

On a recent television show, a man raised in a Christian household decided to see what living like a Muslim was like. He was talking to a leader in the Islamic faith and asked if they believed that Jesus was the Son of God. The Islamic leader stated they thought Jesus was a good man, like Mohammed, or Abraham, but nothing more. At this point, the man could have stated John 10:33, where the Jews state Jesus is claiming to BE God, but he didn't. He just nodded like he agreed, and said "Ok. I see what you mean." He rolled over and kept the show going. I was beside myself with indignation.

No argument.

No fight.

For God, no victory.

I felt like everyone who watched that program was subjected to weak faith and I couldn't make myself watch the program anymore. I turned it off. I don't want to be like that man. Who are you like?

Which Side Will We Choose?

By nature, we're much more like the Joker than Batman. How easy is it to lust or get angry under our breath instead of doing the right thing? It's not that difficult, but we can stop and ask ourselves:

How hard do we fight our sin?

How's our struggle?

Do we struggle, or do we just keep constantly giving in?

Like the Joker, we tend to face problems on our own. We don't need anyone to tell us how to face and fight our woes. We'll get through it just fine. Then we find ourselves sinking deeper and deeper into frustration and sin and can't figure out why we can't get out. We have pushed ourselves so far out to sea, we can't see land anymore. We are on our own... and THAT... is a scary place to be.

What we need to be is like Bruce Wayne. When we have problems, we open up to our "Alfreds," or "Robins." We don't go it alone. And when people try to reach us, we are there, ready to help and fight for the ones we care about. Unafraid to speak the truth.

And so what do we say about the Jokers of the world? Do we say, "Stinks to be you on judgment day..." or condemn them as we see the sin in their lives?

I tell you no.

We have to be like Batman now.

We have to try to reach the Jokers of the world, just like Batman. If they only get one chance, one invitation, one person to care about them, isn't that enough for God? Don't we have to just plant the seed and watch God make it grow if that person is ready? When will that person be ready? We don't know.

But God does.

Because of that, we keep on fighting for them.

Victory after victory, Satan claims another Joker in this world. The chaos that overwhelms them drives them into the prison meant for Satan, not us. We can't be afraid to fight the fight. Not against the Joker, not against man, not against corporations, not against the rich and powerful.

In the big picture, all we need is to remember, every man is just a man. Nothing more... nothing less. We all have the same desires, the same needs in our hearts. We just have to be willing to fight back and have faith that through us, God can accomplish anything.

When we overcome the Joker in our own lives, we can help overcome the Joker in each other's lives.

And that's no joke.

Chapter 21: Epilogue – Batman Beyond

The Future of Gotham

So here we are, at the end.

What else needs to be said? You are ready. Don't doubt yourself. Even in the hardest of times, your perseverance will prove to most that you are the hero you were destined to be.

Your brothers and sisters are your allies. You've been armed with the gifts to reach people around you and help them know that there is a God who exists, loves them, and can do immeasurably more than we could ever hope to accomplish, as long as we have faith. (Ephesians 3:20)

If you've learned anything that has helped you, teach it to others. Batman knew that by spreading his message to just one person he could help the message spread to more people until the city could save itself from its own destruction.

Even in the midst of the hardest times Gotham has faced, Batman never gave up because he knew the city could be saved and become a place of beauty and integrity again.

Maybe your church has lost its zeal.

You be zealous.

Maybe everyone else has given up.

Stand firm.

Perhaps you have dreams for your city spiritually.

Don't give up just because you fall.

We all do at times.

Continuing the Legacy

You may be saying to yourself, "That's Batman. Not me. How can I help anyone the way Batman did, spiritually or otherwise?" There's something I want to show you about the last chapter of Bruce's life, involving a teenager named Terry McGinnis.

Bruce Wayne, though old and retired, in the television show *Batman Beyond*, knew that the world needed a Batman -- a hero that could defend the city against the darkness and inspire others. He found that in a boy named Terry McGinnis, a boy who had lost his father to a corrupt business man who ran Wayne Enterprises.

Bruce saw Terry's anger and lust for vengeance and decided to mentor him, and give him guidance. Teaching Terry the basics of crime-fighting, detective work, and how to use all of his gadgets, he could become the next generation of heroes to challenge the evil heart of the city. Through Bruce's example, Terry learned the difference between revenge and justice, and when confronting his father's killers, decided that justice was better served not through him, but the law he fought to preserve.

In an episode of the Justice League Unlimited television series, coincidentally enough called Epilogue, Terry finds out he is the son of Bruce Wayne. His whole life seemed destined to be a copy of Bruce's down to the tragic loss of his father.

Trying to cope with the shocking truth of this matter, he sought out Amanda Waller, the head of the Cadmus Project. Cadmus was a secret organization that was designed to protect the world from the Justice League, should they go rogue and try to destroy or enslave humanity. Amanda was the only person with the information on how all of this could transpire. He was angry that Bruce would stoop to such levels to ensure his ego lived on.

Amanda soon informs him that it was she who overwrote his father's DNA to that of Bruce's. She saw that Bruce was getting old and soon he would be out of commission or killed. She knew that the world would need a Batman, so she tried to make a new one.

Amanda nearly went as far to hire an assassin to kill Terry's parents at the same age that Bruce lost his parents, but the assassin herself reminded Amanda that Batman wouldn't resort to murder to replace himself and if Amanda was going to honor all that he stood for, neither could she.

So she let Terry's life unfold and as fate would have it, Terry ended up becoming Batman. Watching from afar as he grew up, she knew it would be a matter of time until Terry found the truth.

Terry kept comparing himself to Bruce, but confused, he kept falling short. I know what it's like to come up short when trying to imitate my heroes whether it be Jesus, Batman, or even the people who taught me the scriptures and helped me become a Christian. It can be almost overwhelming trying to live up to someone's expectations and examples.

The key is what Amanda tells Terry next. It's the point I want to get across and it was important enough to save until the end. This is what she had to say:

> *"I've known Bruce Wayne for over fifty years, and I've been keeping an eye on you your whole life. You're not Bruce's clone; you're his son. There are similarities mind you, but more than a few differences too. You don't quite have his magnificent brain for instance; you do have his heart though.*
>
> *And for all that fierce exterior, I've never met anyone who cared as deeply about his fellow man as Bruce Wayne... except maybe you. You want to have a better life than the old man's? Take care of*

the people who love you... or don't. It's your
choice." [r]

There's the key in what she said. We don't have to have Bruce' Wayne's physical perfection. We don't even need to have his money, gadgets, or his intellect. What we can imitate is the hero's heart and the love for our fellow man. In trying to be a spiritual hero, it's all that counts.

What about you? Who around you can you help?

I give you this final charge from the scriptures. A charge amongst heroes. I think it applies appropriately:

> *"Therefore, I urge you, brothers, in view of God's*
> *mercy, to offer your bodies as living sacrifices,*
> *holy and pleasing to God—this is your spiritual act*
> *of worship. Do not conform any longer to the*
> *pattern of this world, but be transformed by the*
> *renewing of your mind. Then you will be able to*
> *test and approve what God's will is—his good,*
> *pleasing and perfect will.*
>
> *For by the grace given me I say to every one of*
> *you: Do not think of yourself more highly than*
> *you ought, but rather think of yourself with sober*
> *judgment, in accordance with the measure of faith*
> *God has given you. Just as each of us has one*
> *body with many members, and these members do*
> *not all have the same function, so in Christ we*
> *who are many form one body, and each member*
> *belongs to all the others. We have different gifts,*
> *according to the grace given us. If a man's gift is*
> *prophesying, let him use it in proportion to his*
> *faith. If it is serving, let him serve; if it is*
> *teaching, let him teach; if it is encouraging, let*
> *him encourage; if it is contributing to the needs of*
> *others, let him give generously; if it is leadership,*
> *let him govern diligently; if it is showing mercy,*
> *let him do it cheerfully.*
>
> *Love must be sincere. Hate what is evil; cling to*
> *what is good. Be devoted to one another in*

brotherly love. Honor one another above yourselves. Never be lacking in zeal, but keep your spiritual fervor, serving the Lord. Be joyful in hope, patient in affliction, faithful in prayer. Share with God's people who are in need. Practice hospitality. Bless those who persecute you; bless and do not curse. Rejoice with those who rejoice; mourn with those who mourn. Live in harmony with one another. Do not be proud, but be willing to associate with people of low position. Do not be conceited.

Do not repay anyone evil for evil. Be careful to do what is right in the eyes of everybody. If it is possible, as far as it depends on you, live at peace with everyone. Do not take revenge, my friends, but leave room for God's wrath, for it is written: "It is mine to avenge; I will repay, "says the Lord. On the contrary: "If your enemy is hungry, feed him; if he is thirsty, give him something to drink.

In doing this, you will heap burning coals on his head. 'Do not be overcome by evil, but overcome evil with good.'"

-Romans 12

All it takes is one man with a vision and faith to change the course of history. You know your enemy. You know your strengths. Fight the good fight and don't give up. You're not a villain and you're better than a bystander.

Have faith in yourself, have faith in others, and finish the race. (1Timothy 6:11-12) Times will arise when everyone around you will long for a hero. A time for someone to shake them out of their apathy and challenge them to their core.

Be that hero.

And when you come face to face with your enemy, don't back down.

Even if all others walk away from you, God is there, cheering you on.

Good luck and God bless you in your journey.

Final Thoughts

This is my second draft of this book and by now, the third installment of Nolan's Dark Knight trilogy is about to hit theaters, I am forced to reflect on my own journey and how I move forward at this stage of my life, which we all do from time to time

I was reading the end of Grant Morrison's tale, the Batman storyline dealing with the death and return of Bruce Wayne, and though Batman's not really dead, the lead-up was actually done rather well.

In the final two Batman issues, Alfred is filling out the last entries of Batman's black case book, which contains all the information he had ever learned throughout all of his superhero career. Since Bruce never came back to finish it, Alfred fills in the last pages. Here's what he wrote:

> *"What they've come to call "Batman's Last Case" was, as you might expect, a mystery **worthy** of his extraordinary talents. It began with a murder of a **god**.*
>
> *I did **once** consider resigning from my position in the Wayne household.*
>
> *"I need a disguise", he said and I thought he'd finally gone mad with grief, especially those next words...*
>
> *...but when I saw what he **meant**, when i **watched** how he surrendred himself to an **ideal**... how he used each **ordeal**, each heartache and failure, to become a **better** man in the service of others... what could I do but stand in humble **awe?** And keep his wounds **clean** and his **uniform** tidy. And send him safely on his way.*
>
> *"I shall become a Bat."*

*"Alfred," he said not long ago. "if anyone ever asks for an **obituary**, tell them the Batman's **Big Secret** was the classic whodunnit?"*

*"Only it's not about who **killed** the Batman but who kept him **alive** all these years." And he **stopped**there, leaving the rest to me.*

*The whereabouts of Batman remain unknown. And yet... I can **see** him now, in the grip of implacable forces, **innumerable** foes. Somewhere without hope. In a place where all seems **lost***

*and i know **this...***

*The enemy will **look away** for just a moment, **underestimating** him for that single fraction of a**second** too long. And no mater how dark the night...*

*...There will be **no hiding place** for Evil. [s]*

What a great final lead up to the finale (supposedly...) of the Caped Crusader's career. I hope the same can be said for my 'career' as a spiritual superhero. In the end though, it really does end up being about the ones who kept us (as heroes) going through the worst of times that should have ended us.

For me it was my grandparents, mostly early on it was my grandmother's care for me, and after her passing, my grandfathers.

I regret that my grandmother wasn't alive to see my growth to where I am or even at my beginning as a Christian, but I know that in the end, at the last of my life, my story should be told that it was never about what finally killed me but who kept me alive and encouraged me to keep going even past their example in this physical world.

For this, I thank my God for my grandparents and their example of what it means to care for your family and fight for what you believe in. To take the step out and do something worthy of remembrance and service to others, pushing past the hard times and growing with each failure, not succumbing to grief.

That's why, as spiritual superheroes, I remember and pledge myself to the charge given to all Spiritual Superheroes in Romans 12.

I really do still miss my grandmother, here almost 15 years after her death. So here I sit, reminded of my fears, but hopeful that all I've fought for is not in vain, but even if it is, my failure will never come in defeats but in doing nothing.

God Bless and encourage us as we take one more day to moving toward the goal of heaven. May we bring as many with us as possible.

-The Spiritual Batman

Eric Gaizat

Appendix 1 - Citations

All citations from Biblical scripture are from the New International Version © 2008 Zondervan Publishing

Chapter 3
[a] Batman: Hush, Volume 1, 2003 , DC Comics, page 6, panel 4

Chapter 4
[b] Batman: Battle for the Cowl, Volume 1, Issue 3, 20, July 2009, DC Comics, page 37, panels 1-5, page 39, panel 1

Chapter 5
[c] Batman, Volume 1, issue 428, 1988, DC Comics, page 2, panels 1-2
[d] Batman: Hush, Volume 2, 2003, DC Comics, page 66, panels 1-3
[e] Batman: Hush, Volume 2, 2003, DC Comics, page 113, panels 1-4 - page 115, panels 6-7

Chapter 6
[f] Batman: Hush, Volume 1, 2003, DC Comics, page 8, panel 1
[g] Batman: Hush, Volume 2, 2003, DC Comics, page 27, panels 3-4, page 28, panel 1, page 29, panel 3, page 30, panels 1-4, page 31, panel 1

Chapter 8
[h] Batman: Under the Red Hood, Volume 1, 2005, DC Comics, page 89, panel 2

Chapter 9
[i] Batman, Volume 1, Issue 397, 1986, DC Comics, page 18, panels 6-7

Chapter 12
[j] Batman, Volume 1, Issue 641, 2005, DC Comics, page 1, panels 5-6, page 2, panel 1

Chapter 15
[k] Batman: Hush, Volume 2, 2003, DC Comics, page 94, panels 6-8

Chapter 16
[l] Batman: Hush Returns, Volume 1, 2006, DC Comics, page 15, panels 4-5

Chapter 18
[m] Batman: Hush, Volume 1, 2003, DC Comics, page 103, panels 3-4

Chapter 19
[n] Batman: Vengeance of Bane, Volume 1, 1992, DC Comics, page 3, panels 4-5

Chapter 20
[o] Batman: The Killing Joke, Volume 1, 1988, DC Comics, page 40, panels 4, 6
[p] Batman: The Killing Joke, Volume 1, 1988, DC Comics, page 5, panels 1, 3, 5
[q] Batman: The Killing Joke, Volume 1, 1988, DC Comics, page 41, panels 2-3

Chapter 21
[r] Justice League Unlimited (2004), Episode 26, Writer Dan Riba, Director Brude Timm & Dwayne McDuffie, July 23, 2005, DC Comics

Final Thoughts
[s] Batman, Volume 1, Issue 683, January 2009, DC Comics, page 32, panel 5, page 33, panels 2-5, page 34, panels 1-5, page 35, panel 1